Survival:

Official Language Rights in Canada

John Richards,
François Vaillancourt,
and William G. Watson

with Marcel Côté and Yvon Fontaine

The Canada Round:
A Series on the Economics of
Constitutional Renewal — No. 10

John McCallum, Series Editor

C.D. Howe Institute

C.D. Howe Institute publications are available from:

Renouf Publishing Company Limited, 1294 Algoma Road,
Ottawa, Ontario K1B 3W8; phone (613) 741-4333; fax (613) 741-5439

and from Renouf's stores at:

61 Sparks Street, Ottawa (613) 238-8985
211 Yonge Street, Toronto (416) 363-3171

For trade book orders, please contact:

McGraw-Hill Ryerson Limited, 300 Water Street,
Whitby, Ontario L1N 9B6; phone (416) 430-5050

Institute publications are also available in microform from:

Micromedia Limited, 165 Hôtel de Ville, Place du Portage, Phase II,
Hull, Quebec J8X 3X2

This book is printed on recycled, acid-free paper.

Canadian Cataloguing in Publication Data

Richards, John
     Survival : official language rights in Canada

(The Canada round ; no. 10)
ISBN 0-88806-302-4

1. Bilingualism – Canada. 2. Canada – Languages –
Law and legislation. 3. Canada – Languages – Political aspects.
4. Quebec (Province) – Languages – Political aspects.
I. Vaillancourt, François. II. Watson, William G.
III. C.D. Howe Institute. IV. Title. V. Series.

KE4413.R53 1992   306.4'46   C92-094021-8

Contents

Foreword

Canada appears poised to embark on an historic political reconfiguration. It is essential that this process be undertaken with a clear and widely diffused understanding of the well-spring of Canadians' economic prosperity.

It is with that in mind that the C.D. Howe Institute presents this series of monographs entitled *The Canada Round*. The series assembles the work of many of Canada's leading economic and political analysts. The monographs are organized into two groups. The first group, called "The Economics of Constitutional Renewal," rests on the assumption of renewed federalism and is organized around economic themes. It examines the economic goals that Canadians have set for themselves, as well as the means of achieving them and the influence of alternative constitutional structures.

The second group of studies, called "The Economics of the Breakup of Confederation," examines the economic consequences of Quebec independence for both Quebec and the rest of Canada. A unique feature of the "Breakup" studies is that they are integrated with the research that has already been carried out by Quebec's Bélanger-Campeau Commission. Where appropriate, each of the studies in this group includes a summary of the relevant analysis by the Bélanger-Campeau Commission, contributions by experts from across Canada, as well as shorter critiques or replies. This format, we believe, will help to pierce Canada's "several solitudes" and create a pan-Canadian meeting of minds.

The Canada Round is not intended to alarm or frighten — the process of collective political definition in this country will turn on more than simply questions of dollars and cents. And, as these monographs will reveal, economics rarely produces an open-and-shut case as to the superiority of one possible set of rules over another. Even if it could do this, it would be unwise to assume that economic analysis alone could change the minds of those who are already committed to a particular vision of the political future.

It is equally clear, however, that Canadians are now seeking a greater understanding of the links between the economy, the Constitution, and legal and political life. A significant reform of the Constitution will influence the economy, in some cases for the better; a rending of the Constitution under conditions of acrimony will almost certainly damage it. Thus, the purpose of the series is to help Canadians think constructively about the benefits and costs of alternative constitutional designs.

Underlying the series is a focus on the economic well-being of Canadians, now and in the future. To best insure this well-being over the short run, Canada needs calm, open negotiations in which efforts are made to understand and incorporate the aspirations of all the participants. This series of monographs is dedicated to that effort.

John McCallum, the series editor and Chairman of the Department of Economics at McGill University, organized the intellectual input. Within the C.D. Howe Institute, David Brown, Senior Policy Analyst, played a coordinating role. This tenth monograph in the series was copy edited by Lenore d'Anjou and Barry A. Norris, and desktop published by Brenda Palmer. As with all C.D. Howe Institute publications, the analysis and views presented here are the responsibility of the authors and do not necessarily reflect the opinions of the Institute's members or Board of Directors.

Thomas E. Kierans
President and
Chief Executive Officer

The Study in Brief

Discussions of language and linguistic minorities are usually difficult, emotional, and potentially controversial. Depending on their viewpoints and backgrounds, those who comment on a subject such as this tend to approach it with widely varying assumptions that are not always explicit. So the introduction by Marcel Côté to this volume of "The Canada Round" is particularly useful, as he adds perspective to the debate and shows the reader where each of the contributors is coming from.

John Richards, going back to the recommendations of the 1979 federal Task Force on Canadian Unity, chaired by Jean-Luc Pepin and John Robarts, presents a forceful argument for provincial jurisdiction over language. While the rights of linguistic minorities would enjoy the protection of the Charter of Rights and Freedoms and federal policies promoting bilingualism would continue, provinces would otherwise be free to legislate on language as they saw fit. No longer would statutes of the Western provinces be translated into French, and Quebec's language laws would operate with greater legitimacy than they enjoy today. Richards sees this recommendation as an alternative — or perhaps an addition — to a "distinct society" clause in the Constitution. If distinct society fails, the federal government might instead advocate provincial jurisdiction over language.

Richards presents two principal arguments for his case. First, history shows that people attach great importance to the preservation of their language. If the distinct society clause runs into trouble, then the failure to grant Quebec jurisdiction over language is to risk either the province's separation or its descent into the Irish model. Second, the economics of language provide a firm moral argument to counter those who maintain that free choice on language is a fundamental civil right. The basic economic point is that there are important external effects: additional speakers of a language create a communication benefit for others who speak that language. Generally speaking, this means that the minor language will gradually disappear whenever there is a free market in language. Hence, advocates of linguistic free choice are in fact saying that it would be morally acceptable for Montreal to become, in time, a majority anglophone city even if most Quebecers opposed this outcome intensely.

François Vaillancourt marshalls a statistical summary of trends in the use of French in Quebec and patterns of migration to show that, in recent decades, francophone Quebecers have made great strides in several areas: the use of French in the workplace, the proportion of the population going to French schools, francophone control over the economy, and relative income levels of francophones and anglophones. Partly using the same economic arguments that Richards advances, Vaillancourt then recommends policies to promote French as the language of internal communication in Quebec. To achieve this objective, he argues, businesses and public and private organizations operating in the Quebec market should be able to serve their Quebec clientele in French at all times. He also presents a series of policy recommendations concerning the language of education, signs, and so on.

William Watson begins by describing the reasons Quebec anglophones might leave if Quebec separates. These include a straightforward attachment to Canada, fears of economic loss in an independent Quebec, and concerns that traditional anglophone rights might not be respected. He then goes on to enumerate the negative economic consequences of large-scale emigration for those Quebecers who remain behind. Assuming the francophone majority would want anglophones to stay, Watson asks what measures the government of a newly independent Quebec could take to help achieve this objective. In general, he argues, the most important action would be to offer firm guarantees to the anglophone population regarding their linguistic rights and their institutions — schools, hospitals, universities, and so on. The Quebec Charter of Rights, he says, would not provide a firm guarantee because it could be changed by an act of the National Assembly. Instead, he suggests, an independent Quebec should set up constitutional guarantees that would be difficult for subsequent governments to change. One possibility is a "federalism-in-Quebec" system, whereby constitutional changes in particular areas would require the agreement of several of Quebec's regions or communities.

The volume also contains comments by Watson on Vaillancourt and Vaillancourt on Watson. There is little common ground between the two: Watson criticizes Vaillancourt for authoritarian tendencies, while Vaillancourt comments that if Quebec were to become independent, francophones would be unlikely to want to share their newly acquired sovereignty with anglophones.

John McCallum
Series Editor

Language and Public Policy

Marcel Côté

For bilingual countries, finding the proper linguistic balance is a fundamental challenge that propels language policies to the top of the political agenda. Moreover, the linguistic debate in bilingual countries is often at the forefront of the nationalist conflict. Indeed, language is often the privileged theater of battle for separatist forces. Canada is no exception in that regard.

The three papers in this study provide a good overview of the Canadian (and Quebec) language predicament. John Richards presents a comprehensive review of the issue. In his search for the evanescent ideal balance between the linguistic rights of French- and English-speaking Canadians, he presents a compelling argument for assigning constitutional jurisdiction over language to the provinces.

Bill Watson is an English-speaking Montrealer. He assesses the future of anglophone Quebecers in an independent Quebec, why many of them would leave, the economic effects of this emigration, and the conditions under which it could be minimized.

In many ways, François Vaillancourt's proposal for linguistic policies in Quebec is at the other end of the political spectrum, centered as much on the interests of francophones as Watson's analysis deals with anglophone Quebecers' point of view. Vaillancourt's perspective is dual, in that he is both an *indépendantiste* and an analytical economist specializing in human capital. Both traits underlay his argumentation for a language policy suited for a *Québec français*.

Finding a New Balance

John Richard's paper illustrates the classic Canadian search for balance between the concerns of the country's two linguistic groups.

His proposal to assign the constitutional responsibility of language to the provinces allows for a differential treatment of linguistic situations, which vary greatly across the land. In particular, the situation of French as a minority language in North America is quite different from that of English as a minority language in Quebec. As a safeguard for linguistic minorities, Richards would also enshrine linguistic rights in the Charter of Rights and Freedoms.

One of the merits of assigning jurisdiction over language to the provinces is that it would make the "distinct society" concept in the Constitution somewhat redundant. If this had been done in the *Constitution Act, 1982*, it would have avoided the divisive debate on the meaning and reach of such a clause that was central to many Canadians' rejection of the Meech Lake Accord. Richards' proposal, originally developed by the federal Task Force on Canadian Unity (the Pepin-Robarts Commission) in the late 1970s, is based on the presumption that linguistic minorities will be well treated by provincial authorities both in Quebec and in the rest of Canada. As Yvon Fontaine points out in his comments on Richards' paper, however, the English-speaking minority in Quebec and French-speaking minorities outside Quebec would have reservations about such an arrangement, despite the protection that the Charter could offer. Moreover, it is unlikely that Quebec nationalists, who are very influential in the debate on language policies in that province, would agree to enshrining in the Charter a strong protection of English-language rights in Quebec.

It is also far from certain that francophone Quebecers would abandon the distinct society as a constitutional must. In the short span of ten years, the inclusion of a distinct society clause in the Constitution has become for Quebecers a symbol of the official recognition of the special character of Quebec. Deleting it would be perceived as a rejection of this recognition. Thus, it is unlikely that we can turn the clock back to 1982 and start anew with a different approach to the constitutional treatment of language. Introducing exclusive provincial jurisdiction over language may just add another level of complexity to the constitutional tangle.

Nevertheless, over time, this avenue could lead Canada to a much more serene management of its linguistic duality. Internationally, the territorial approach to linguistic policy in bilingual countries is becoming the norm. Regional minorities tend to be against territoriality, mainly because the political coalitions supporting minority rights tend to be weaker on a regional basis. In Canada, the historical abridgment of the linguistic rights of minorities by provincial governments fuels a deep mistrust. But Canada is becoming a society in which the exercise of individual rights is increasingly promoted by the judicial system. Charter protection would ensure that this would continue to be the case in Canada. Moreover, whenever minority rights are involved, regional politics fall under the national limelight, making it politically harder to limit the rights of linguistic minorities. Thus, it may be time for Canada to move toward a territorial approach to linguistic policy.

Bill Watson's Quebec

After all the fuss over Quebec's language legislation of the past two decades, one can still observe as much English on signs on St. Catherine Street in Montreal,[1] as French on signs on Rideau Street in Ottawa. Both streets are the main commercial thoroughfares of regions in which linguistic minorities comprise about 30 percent of the population. Moreover, English is probably spoken more frequently in the shops on St. Catherine Street than French is in the shops on Rideau Street. The two streets present a mirror image of Canada's linguistic duality in day-to-day usage. In Ottawa, the balance is maintained by market forces. In Montreal, the balance is maintained by government intervention.

Watson would prefer that market forces prevail in Montreal, but this will probably never be the case. Whenever unimpeded market forces yield a politically unpalatable state of affairs, government

---

1 Quebec's language legislation has more loopholes than is generally assumed. For instance, federally regulated banks and federal government offices still enforce a strict policy of bilingualism on their public signs.

intervention is usually the result. Public policy offers countless examples: Watson's home is protected from the vulgar greed of apartment builders by government zoning regulations, which constrain the working of the market place.

Language usage involves what economists call "externalities." The receptor often has little control over the language that is thrust into his or her eyes and ears, and this can be a major source of irritation. Many francophone Quebecers react to English-language billboards in the same way others react to highway billboards. They are seen as encroachments into the fragile "French" space in North America, and what for nonfrancophones appears to be intolerance is for francophones a deep-seated reaction to a cultural threat.

Language is also a public good. Accepting the use of a second language in that regard diminishes the value of that common good for those who speak only one language. But any restriction on the use of a language becomes a question of fundamental rights. Freedom of speech gets dragged in and, ultimately, so do Supreme Court judges.

In the final analysis, linguistic policies have to pass a test of political acceptance. Over the years, political pressures have pushed successive Quebec governments to legislate restrictions on the public use of English. Are Quebec's present language policies — in particular, the restrictions on sign language and for the school of choice for immigrants — unacceptable? By the same token, are the "linguistic packages" offered to francophones in other provinces acceptable? Patterns of outmigration by linguistic minorities are indications of acceptability. But language policies are only one element in the larger political debate involving the coexistence of francophones and anglophones in the area. It is thus difficult to isolate the specific role of language policy.

Watson goes beyond the discomforts of Quebec's language policies and assesses the attitudes of anglophone Quebecers if the province were to separate. He makes clear that many of them, and many "allophones," will choose to leave, at great cost to the Quebec economy. He is probably right. The secession of Quebec as viewed from the perspective of an anglophone is very different from that of a francophone. The resulting personal behavior of each is also likely to be quite different, something which most *indépendantistes* refuse to admit, probably because the economic consequences would not be too pleasant for those who stay.[2]

Francophone Quebecers generally believe that anglophones are well treated in Quebec, and will be well treated in a postindependence Quebec. Flicking TV channels in Montreal tells it all: access to English is unimpeded. And the anglophone minority's control over its school and health-care systems is unquestioned. So what is the worry? Why do some anglophones find it so wrong to ensure that the face of Quebec be French, with constraints on the use of English on signs?

Such generalized attitudes ensure that most Quebec francophones will not believe Watson's analysis of the calculus of anglophone Quebecers if secession comes. Unfortunately, the economic consequences of a significant emigration of anglophones and allophones in the shaky period following secession are not to be discarded lightly, as Watson's analysis points out.

Many francophones will also be irritated by Watson's discussion of the conditions that would prevent such large-scale emigration if Quebec were to secede. Most would agree with the obvious, such as enshrining in a Quebec constitution the rights that the anglophone minority now enjoys. But some of Watson's other musings, such as running the boundary of Quebec down the middle of Peel Street, will antagonize many readers and undermine his credibility. For most francophone Quebecers, the territorial integrity of Quebec, as presently defined, is sacred — a not-surprising attitude for a people who consider themselves a threatened minority.

Yet, after reading Vaillancourt on the role of English and anglophones in Quebec — whether or not it becomes independent — one

---

2 Indeed, Vaillancourt's flimsy disregard for Watson's point of view is typical. The *indépendantiste* discourse does not allow much room for costs resulting from the emigration of unhappy anglophone Quebecers, which is deemed to be a relatively insignificant phenomenon. As Vaillancourt illustrates well, *indépendantistes* focus on past wrongs.

cannot be but sympathetic to Watson's worries about the future of the rights of the English-speaking minority. Vaillancourt's cool consideration of "the wholesale compulsory transfer of non-French-speaking people from Quebec to [the rest of Canada]," and his dismissal of such a policy because it is neither advocated nor likely to happen, despite the experience of Europe after World War II, is not reassuring.

The *Québec français* Approach

François Vaillancourt's analysis rests on a fundamental premise that can be called *Québec français*: Quebec is "a French country." In this conceptual framework, the English language has no "right" to exist in Quebec, only usefulness. And there is no recognition of English-speaking Quebecers: there are only Quebecers in Quebec, and all Quebecers are expected to speak French and to be culturally at ease in *Québec français*. In other words, Quebec, and Montreal in particular, is as French as Paris is French or London is English. Anglophone and allophone Quebecers should assimilate or leave.

Squaring this premise with the facts is the objective of Vaillancourt's policy prescriptions. The first part of his paper aims at demonstrating that Quebec is slowly getting there. But his data also indicate that Quebec is not yet French. For proponents of *Québec français*, the present pace of change is not sufficient, and more radical linguistic policy is warranted.

In the second part of his paper, Vaillancourt proposes a set of policies to achieve this blissful state of affairs. The strategy underlying its approach is as simple as its premise: Legislate the "reality" that Quebec is a French enclave in the North American economic space, force the use of French as the common language, and ensure that all Quebecers are fluent in French. The strategy should also minimize the costs of managing the linguistic interface with English-speaking North America and, as a consequence, it allows for a liberal use of English, whenever the economic reality dictates it.

Vaillancourt represents a minority point of view in Quebec. Indeed, his view is disputed even among *indépendantistes*. The crux of the debate centers on the historical rights of anglophone Quebecers — in particular, whether they have the right to use their language publicly — in a society in which most people would prefer French to be the common language. Most francophone Quebecers do not deny that English-speaking Quebecers, whose roots in Quebec date back 200 years, are as much Quebecers as they are.

Thus, to what extent can linguistic coexistence can be allowed? Most francophone Quebecers are happy with the present state of affairs, which includes restrictions on the use of English on public signs and which channels the children of immigrants to the French school system. Although they are very unhappy with the restrictions on individual rights implicit in the sign regulations, most English-speaking Quebecers also accept the present situation, if it is to end a debate for which they have less and less enthusiasm.

Vaillancourt defends the hard-line *Québec français* position. Deep down, its proponents want to undo 1760 and the Plains of Abraham and to assert the absolute French character of all the territory of Quebec. This should not, however, be construed as their wanting to turn back the clock: they are quite liberal concerning the use of English, but as a second language. Indeed, they argue that all Quebecers should learn to speak English.

This position leaves many francophone Quebecers ill at ease. A solid majority of them respects the historical rights of English-speaking Quebecers to live in Quebec as English-speaking people, with their own institutions and their own communities, despite occasional disagreements about where the line should be drawn. Quebecers will also be astonished by the huge cost of *Québec français*. As Vaillancourt candidly points out, the virtual reality of *Québec français* comes with a hefty price tag — up to 15 or 20 percent of personal income. Even if this estimate is on the high side, it will not fly politically. And political acceptance remains the ultimate arbiter in a democracy.

An Endemic Debate

In several ways, linguistic duality is both a blessing and a curse for Canada. It is at the root of tensions that threaten the very existence of the country. Indeed, many Canadians on both sides of the linguistic divide have had enough. But Canada's linguistic duality is one of its most distinctive traits, and sharing two cultures greatly enriches the experience of being Canadian. Managing this duality is Canada's greatest political challenge, however, and whether or not Canadians like it, the language issue will fuel the Canadian constitutional debate forever.

The Case for an Explicit Division of Powers over Language

John Richards

We Canadians are not unique in facing difficulties over the constitutional treatment of language; it is a frequent source of controversy in multilingual states. Eduard Shevardnadze, former Soviet minister of foreign affairs and before that first secretary of the Georgian Communist Party, has related the task of rewriting the Georgian constitution:

> I will never forget the dramatic passage of the new Georgian Constitution at the April 1978 session of the republic's Supreme Soviet. The majority demanded the retention of the article that made Georgian the republic's official language....But the status had been omitted from the new draft at the behest of government legal experts in Moscow, who claimed that the "article contradicts Marxism-Leninism."
>
> I expressed my concern about this to Brezhnev [and others]....
>
> It was not easy to convince them that it was unwise to remove the article on the official language....On the day of the Supreme Soviet session, several hours before it opened, I had a telephone conversation with Suslov [then head of ideology on the Politburo],...reminded him of [the nationalist demonstrations in Tbilisi in] 1956, tried to persuade him, and finally said that I would act at my own discretion....
>
> We prevented a great tragedy and adopted a Constitution in conformity with the will of the people.[2]

I thank Allan Blakeney and John McCallum for thoughtful criticisms of earlier drafts of this paper. As is traditional, all responsibility for the remaining inadequacies is mine, not theirs.

1 Eduard Shevardnadze, *The Future Belongs to Freedom* (London: Sinclair-Stevenson, 1991), pp. 34–35.

The parallel — between Shevardnadze's frustration in attempting to explain to Muscovites the importance to Georgians of constitutional guarantees for their language and the frustration of Québécois[2] politicians in attempting to explain to Canadians in "the Rest of Canada" (ROC) the analogous demands by most Québécois on behalf of guarantees for French within their province — needs little elaboration. In a poll conducted in October 1991, 63 percent of Quebec residents supported the federal government's proposal to recognize Quebec as a "distinct society"; only 29 percent opposed it. Among ROC residents, the results were almost exactly the reverse: 63 percent opposed; 28 percent approved.[3] A second poll conducted a month later confirmed the divergent attitudes. In Quebec, it found 77 percent supportive of the distinct society clause and 20 percent opposed; in ROC, 69 percent were opposed and 28 percent supportive.[4]

A second parallel between the former Soviet Union and Canada is the growing importance of conflicting nationalist movements — in Georgia and other republics, in Quebec and other provinces. In moderation, nationalism is a healthy affirmation of community, but nationalist dialogues frequently slide from an affirmation of community into a simplistic condemnation of outsiders as the basic cause of domestic political problems. This attitude has arisen in many republics of the former Soviet Union, including Georgia. On a less dramatic level, Canada faces analogous problems. The embrace by particular groups of Canadians of conflicting nationalist dialogues has rendered constitutional reconciliation within a federal framework exceedingly difficult. To continue with poll data, a majority of those in ROC opposed to the distinct society clause were so adamant

2   I use "Québécois" to refer to francophone residents of Quebec. Use of this shorthand does not imply that nonfrancophone Quebec residents are any less legitimate citizens of the province.

3   "Canadians Cool to Proposals for New Constitution," *Globe and Mail* (Toronto), November 4, 1991.

4   "Cross-Canada Opinions: *Maclean's*/Decima Poll," *Maclean's*, January 6, 1992.

that they were not willing to accept it as a compromise even if its rejection meant the breakdown of constitutional negotiations.[5]

I write, nonetheless, in the belief that it is still desirable and politically feasible to reconcile. To do so will require a greater spirit of compromise than Canadians have demonstrated recently. It will require that we neither embrace uncritically nor condemn uncritically the various constitutional demands in circulation — that we be prepared to separate the kernels of political wisdom from the chaff of political rhetoric. We can accept the value of entrenching a general statement on the desirability of aboriginal exercise of self-government without embracing the extreme aboriginal case about white racism. We can admit there are good reasons to favor an elected Senate without embracing the populist nationalism of the Reform Party. We can favor a modest social charter without embracing the left-wing nationalism promoted by many of its advocates. We can support recognition of the Quebec government's role in preserving and promoting French within the province without embracing *pur et dur* Quebec nationalism.

On this final dimension of constitutional debate, Marcel Côté, a prominent political consultant, has succinctly captured the core of the argument:

> Some say Québécois are inconsistent because polls have shown fluctuating proportions who favor outright independence, sovereignty-association, or some form of federalism. But that is not so. We have been remarkably consistent over the past decade. A quarter of us have supported Trudeau's concept of a centralized federation; a quarter have supported outright independence. The half in the middle have wanted to remain Canadians provided Quebec remains French. For this group, what has fluctu-

---

5 According to the *Globe and Mail* poll (see footnote 3), 63 percent of Canadians in ROC oppose any distinct society clause. Of this 63 percent, a majority (56 percent) are unwilling to compromise on their opposition. The analogous statistics from the *Maclean's*/Decima poll (see footnote 4) are that 69 percent in ROC are opposed, and of that 69 percent, 56 percent are not willing to compromise. (See footnote 21 for the wording of the questions.)

ated is primarily faith in the willingness of Canadians outside
Quebec to accept the legitimacy of our acting to preserve our
language and culture.[6]

Some anglophones have captured the argument with equal precision. An example is Robert Stanfield, former premier of Nova Scotia
and former leader of the federal Conservatives:

> I...wonder whether, if Quebecers were reassured about the fu-
> ture of their distinct society, its preservation might cease to be
> the dominant factor in their voting. Thus reassured, Quebec
> might well develop voting patterns similar to those in other
> regions.
>
> Of course there are good reasons for the Québécois to want
> constitutional protection to preserve and strengthen their dis-
> tinct society. They see themselves swimming in an ocean of
> English in North America. They know that French is even more
> vulnerable than it used to be. They know that the modernization
> of Quebec increased the pressure from English, which is the
> language of society and technology, of North American enter-
> tainment and modern communication.
>
> While some of the measures taken in Quebec to protect
> French may seem of doubtful value, one can hardly doubt the
> reality of the threat to French, the language Quebecers have
> fought to preserve for more than two centuries.
>
> Those of us who are not Quebecers should be able to under-
> stand that. Far from hurting the country as a whole, a vigorous
> French language and culture in Quebec gives Canada an addi-
> tional dimension.[7]

Plan of the Essay

In outline, this essay proceeds as follows. The first section summarizes linguistic trends in Quebec and ROC. In the next section,

---

6 Free translation from several talks; M. Côté has approved this translation.

7 R. Stanfield, "Canada *sans* Quebec Just a Pale U.S. Image," *Globe and Mail*
   (Toronto), December 16, 1991, p. A19. The article was adapted from a speech at
   the University of Ottawa.

I examine three principles on which multilingual federations base language policy. In the third section, I make a general case for decentralized jurisdiction over language. Finally, I discuss the relative merits of drafting constitutional changes in terms of "distinct society" or in terms of the recommendation of the Pepin-Robarts Report[8] that jurisdiction over language be explicitly divided between the federal and provincial levels of government. I believe the latter approach would prove less controversial in both Quebec and ROC.

Trends in Language in Canada

Before we can assess linguistic options in the current constitutional impasse, we must appreciate what has actually happened to the use of language by Canadians. The following seven points provide a minimum summary. (See Appendix A for somewhat more detailed data.)[9]

1. Quebec has remained overwhelmingly French-speaking throughout the twentieth century, but the proportion of francophone Canadians has declined since 1951.

Outside the Greater Montreal area, francophones[10] constituted about 94 percent of the Quebec population in 1986; in the province as a whole, they comprised 83 percent. Between 1931 and 1951, francophones increased their relative weight within the province and within the country as a whole. The dramatic decline in the Québécois birth rate contributed to a post-1951 decline in the francophone share of the Canadian population; by 1986, it had fallen to 25 percent. Within Quebec, however, this decline in fertility was

---

8 Canada, Task Force on Canadian Unity, *A Future Together*, co-chaired by Jean-Luc Pepin and John Robarts (Ottawa: Supply and Services Canada, 1979).

9 Appendix A is the immediate source for all the statistics in this section.

10 "Francophone" is defined by mother tongue (language used in family of origin) unless otherwise indicated.

more than offset after 1971 by a combination of net out-of-province emigration of anglophones and allophones and a relatively small net immigration of them from abroad.

2.   French is an increasingly marginal language in ROC. Virtually all ROC communities in which French is the language of use are restricted to eastern Ontario and New Brunswick, the bilingual belts adjacent to Quebec.

In terms of mother tongue, the proportion of francophones in ROC declined from 7 percent in 1931 to 5 percent in 1986. In terms of language of use, the decline was greater, indicating significant assimilation to English. Of the slightly less than 1 million Canadians outside Quebec whose mother tongue is French, nearly three-quarters live in eastern Ontario and northern New Brunswick. By language of use, francophones in 1986 comprised 31 percent of New Brunswickers and 3 percent of Ontarians but scarcely more than 1 percent of the population of the seven remaining provinces. The combination of federal plus provincial support for bilingualism has stabilized the francophone share of New Brunswick's population. In all other provinces, the relative benefits of learning English, as opposed to French, far outweigh any subsidies directed toward the francophone minorities.

3.   Quebec's anglophone community has declined; the rate of decline accelerated in the 1970s.

The anglophone community has been historically important in Quebec since the late eighteenth century. Since the 1960s, however, it has lost much of its economic and political power in the province, and in the past two decades the Quebec government has introduced legislation to promote French and restrict use of English, inducing significant anglophone emigration from the province. In the middle four decades of this century, the anglophone community declined slowly, from 15 percent of the Quebec total in 1931 to 13 percent by 1971; it declined much more rapidly during the next 15 years, to 10 percent by 1986.

4. In Quebec, the allophone[11] community is proportionately smaller than in ROC, but its relative importance has increased in recent years, particularly in Montreal.

Until the 1980s, allophones in Quebec assimilated to English, as opposed to French, in ratios of more than two to one. This trend has been reversed for more recent immigrants. In Montreal, the anglophone and allophone communities are now of approximately equal size.

5. In ROC, allophones in aggregate outnumber francophones by a ratio of three to one.

Among the ROC provinces, allophones outnumber francophones in all except the three Maritime provinces. In the four Western provinces, allophones outnumber francophones by nearly seven to one.

6. In Montreal, the shifts in the relative size of the city's linguistic communities have been large during the past half-century but have coincidentally left the proportion of francophones unchanged at approximately 63 percent.

Preservation and promotion of the French character of Montreal has always been at the heart of Québécois linguistic concerns. The second-largest francophone city in the world is on the frontier between a small francophone hinterland and an immensely larger anglophone one. At times in the nineteenth century, the city contained an anglophone majority. During the past 50 years, the growth of allophone communities has almost exactly balanced the emigration of anglophones. These volatile shifts in linguistic communities indicate the potential for large shifts in the city's linguistic character.

7. The knowledge of French among nonfrancophones in Quebec has increased since 1931; the rise since 1971 has been particularly dramatic. The knowledge of French among nonfrancophones in ROC has also increased, but it remains negligibly small.

---

11 "Allophone" is defined as any member of a linguistic minority whose mother tongue is neither French nor English.

Many anglophone Quebecers and allophone immigrants who originally settled in Quebec have left the province. Among those who have remained, the proportion speaking French increased from 40 percent in 1971 to 62 percent in 1986. The emergence of a non-francophone population that is, in its majority, bilingual is a remarkable new phenomenon for Quebec. Conversely, the fraction of non-anglophones in Quebec able to speak English has remained constant at one-third for the past half-century. Federal bilingual policies have had only a minute effect on increasing knowledge of French among nonfrancophones in ROC; the proportion claiming to speak French rose from 4 to 6 percent between 1971 and 1986.

Linguistic Policies

Given the linguistic situation just described, I argue for an explicit division of powers over language jurisdiction, creating domains for both federal and provincial jurisdiction. Such a division of powers should in no way preclude Ottawa from pursuing bilingualism within its jurisdiction.

Alternative Principles

Three principles — in theory, alternative principles — can govern language policy within multilingual federations. One is an explicit division of powers just mentioned. A second is for the central state to seek to impose the major language over minor languages, on grounds that linguistic uniformity will contribute to political unity. The result of such policy has frequently been the exact opposite. Advocates of Russification of the Soviet republics contributed to alienation from Moscow. Indian nationalists have weakened the authority of New Delhi by seeking to impose Hindi throughout the country. Although it is doubtful that any aboriginal languages spoken in Canada (all of which were without written form) could have survived extensive contact with European languages after European settlement, state-accelerated assimilation — via, for example, the early refusal of Indian Affairs schools to teach aboriginal languages — has exacerbated resentment among aboriginal peoples.

Another principle on which to base language policy is to consider it an extension of individual civil liberties: individuals should have the right to use the language of their choice, and the state should not intervene. This principle has an obvious appeal in a liberal pluralist society.

In Canada, we currently apply all three of these principles:

Division of power. The Quebec government asserts *de facto* division of power over language. Since the Catholic Church stopped being the leading defender of *la langue et la foi* in the 1960s, Quebec governments have legislated to reinforce the role of French as the dominant language in Quebec. The most important aspects are the regulations on French as the language of instruction and in the workplace. Bill 101 limits access to English schooling to children whose parents are Canadian citizens who received their education in Canada in English. It also requires major firms to obtain *certificats de francisation*, showing satisfactory levels of utilization of French. In addition, passing an examination showing competence in French is a requirement for many professional licenses.

Imposition. Both the central and the provincial governments effectively impose the official languages on immigrant communities speaking languages other than French or English. Most immigrants have chosen to come to Canada to escape political persecution or poor economic prospects in their homeland. They accept that learning to function in a new language is a necessary cost of migration. Less willingly, they acquiesce to intergenerational loss of familiarity with their original language. Where their numbers warrant, they nonetheless seek political influence to preserve and promote their original language as a second language.

Free choice. The federal government treats the choice between the official languages as an individual civil liberty. Various statutes — including sections of the original *British North America (BNA) Act*, the *Official Languages Act*, and the Charter of Rights and Freedoms — are based on this principle. So that individuals could exercise linguistic choices meaningfully, the federal government, under Lester Pearson and Pierre Trudeau in the 1960s and 1970s, imposed much more explicit duties on the federal government to provide bilingual services. It also generously subsidized the provision of minority language services in the domain of provincial jurisdiction — French services in ROC, English in Quebec. Given the evolution of Quebec policies, however, Ottawa's support of Quebec's anglophone minority has been largely ineffective; given the forces affecting intergenerational linguistic choice, Ottawa's support of francophone minorities in ROC has not been much more effective.

A society can tolerate a measure of discordance between reality and official principles. In no functioning state does actual policy neatly follow one of the three possible principles. Canadian language policies in aggregate, however, are so manifestly incompatible and ambiguous that they have engendered cynicism, confusion, and anger. The long, complex saga of Canadian language policy, from the *Quebec Act* to the Meech Lake Accord, makes obvious that linguistic conflicts have arisen elsewhere in Canada, and not only in Quebec. Each battlefield requires description.

Quebec

Québécois are hostile to federal bilingualism and the Charter of Rights as restrictions on Quebec's linguistic jurisdiction. The province's anglophones and allophones oppose what they perceive as the Quebec government's violation of their right of free choice between French and English.

The *Official Languages Act* of 1969 and the 1982 Charter refer to French and English as the official languages of Canada. The authors of these documents hoped for an environment in which the official language minorities — anglophones in Quebec and francophones in ROC — would be treated equally. They implied to these minorities that they enjoyed strong — ultimately justiciable — linguistic rights that amounted to virtual free choice throughout the country. Inspired by the Charter, anglophones in Quebec launched a court challenge (*Ford v. Attorney General of Quebec*) of the unilingual sign provisions of Bill 101. The Supreme Court's 1988 ruling on this case revealed the profound disagreement between Québécois and virtually all other Canadians on this matter. The court found Bill 101's unilingual commercial sign provisions to be in violation of rights of freedom of expression accorded under both the Quebec and federal charters.[12] The Quebec government utilized the "notwithstanding clause" of the Canadian Charter (section 33) to override the Supreme Court and impose a compromise (Bill 178) that allowed bilingual signs inside commercial establishments but preserved unilingualism outside.

Non-Québécois reacted with spontaneous hostility to Quebec's resort to the notwithstanding clause, on the grounds that it violated individual linguistic rights. The passage of Bill 178 rendered remote the possibility of securing the required unanimous endorsement of the Meech Lake Accord by all ten provincial legis- latures, and within 18 months that attempt at constitutional compromise was dead.[13]

Following defeat of the Parti Québécois referendum in 1980, most journalistic and academic observers[14] had thought Québécois nationalism would be in decline for a generation. They were clearly wrong. The Supreme Court decision on unilingual signs convinced Québécois that the constitutional basis for their language regime was no stronger than the notwithstanding clause — a fortuitous loophole in the Charter, introduced at the insistence of Western premiers

---

12 See M. Mandel, *The Charter of Rights and the Legalization of Politics in Canada* (Toronto: Wall & Thompson, 1989).

13 At the time of the Supreme Court's unilingual sign ruling, the accord had been endorsed by eight of ten provincial legislatures — all except those of Manitoba and New Brunswick. Clyde Wells' Liberals rescinded Newfoundland's former endorsation in April 1990. During the last death agonies of the accord in June 1990, the governments of New Brunswick, Newfoundland, and Manitoba submitted the accord to their legislatures. New Brunswick approved it; procedural opposition prevented Manitoba legislators from voting; and Newfoundland legislators also failed to conduct a vote.

14 See, for example, D.V. Smiley, *The Federal Condition in Canada* (Toronto: McGraw-Hill Ryerson, 1987).

anxious to preserve a measure of parliamentary supremacy. More fundamentally, the political furor in opposition to Bill 178 and, in turn, to the distinct society clause of the Meech Lake Accord revealed the political fragility of their position and gave renewed credibility to the *pur et dur* nationalist argument that only in an independent Quebec would French be secure.

Hostility among Quebec's anglophones and allophones to the province's language policy was sufficiently strong in the wake of Bill 178 to break their long-standing commitment to the Quebec Liberal Party. The new Equality Party emerged, explicitly championing language policy based on individual freedom of choice and support for the federal Charter. Its members typically favor partition of Quebec, should it separate, preserving for Canada those areas where English is the majority language: northern Quebec (dominated by aboriginals) and the western half of the Island of Montreal, which make up the larger part of Quebec's present territory. The success of the Equality Party — it won four seats in the provincial general election of 1989 — crystallizes the differences between opposing principles for language policy and complicates the negotiation of compromises among Quebec's linguistic communities.

The Rest of Canada

The majority of nonfrancophones in ROC view the pursuit of federal bilingual policies as largely symbolic and ineffective in preventing assimilation of ROC francophones. Allophones, who greatly outnumber francophones in ROC, perceive such policies as excessive public subsidy of one linguistic minority over all others. And many people from every linguistic group see the situation as unjust inasmuch as Quebec does not treat its linguistic minorities in an analogous manner.

In ROC, the majority of anglophones and allophones clearly accept official bilingualism within the federal jurisdiction, but they simultaneously believe it has been extended too far at the behest of francophones. Outside the Maritimes, francophones are outnumbered by members of allophone communities. Furthermore, federal bilingualism invites the critique that francophones are hypocrites — sending politicians to Ottawa to advance bilingualism on behalf of francophones in ROC while sending politicians to Quebec City to restrict use of English in "their" province. Although some part of this criticism is probably motivated by cultural intolerance, there is an undeniable logic to the charge that francophones want to have their cake and eat it too.

Francophones in ROC are predictably ambivalent. On the one hand, many favor Quebec's language policy on the grounds that a secure francophone bastion is required if they themselves are to survive linguistically. On the other hand, they are the immediate beneficiaries of the federal subsidy of official language minorities and favor continuation of such subsidy.

Another Parallel

There is a depressingly close parallel between the Quebec Question, which has haunted Canadian politics since the 1960s, and the Irish Question, which haunted British politics for 50 years prior to creation of the Irish Free State in 1922. "Home Rule" became the central demand of constitutional Irish nationalists in the 1880s. Their support was critical to Gladstone's Liberals; he endorsed the principle and, in 1886, introduced a Home Rule Bill into Parliament. It was defeated when a minority of his own caucus supported the Conservatives, who championed imperial unity. In conjunction with the Protestant Unionists of Northern Ireland — who equated Home Rule" to "Rome rule" — the Conservatives then defeated the Liberals at the polls and, as the government, refused to compromise with Irish nationalists.

Over the years, moderate Irish nationalists gave way to the more militant, who adamantly claimed sovereignty for all of Ireland. Irish Protestants, a majority in the six northern counties, became ever more hostile to Irish nationalism and clung ever more tenaciously to the link with Britain. Both sides committed acts of wanton violence, and by the end of World War I, Britain ruled the 26 southern counties as an occupying military force.

It is devoutly to be hoped that Canada can avoid the final stages of this historical precedent, which still resonates in Northern Ireland today.

The Case for Provincial Jurisdiction over Language

The case for explicit division of powers over language, decentralizing important domains to the provinces — to Quebec, in particular — can be argued from at least three perspectives: pragmatism, external effects, and avoidance of discrimination.[15]

The Argument from Realpolitik

The first argument for decentralized jurisdiction is pragmatic. People are not willing to strike deals on other dimensions of political life when they feel their linguistic community is endangered. In such circumstances, they usually rank language over economics. This has been true of Québécois. It applies equally to the citizens of various republics within the former Soviet Union, to several linguistic communities in Western Europe — for example, the Flemish, the Walloons, and the Catalans — and to several non-Hindi communities of India.

That people place great importance on the preservation of language is one of the few really robust empirical generalizations about political activity. Language is important to everyone, and preservation or promotion of language is at the core of virtually all nationalist movements. People have other political goals besides

---

15 Two important articles addressing the issue of alternate principles on which to base language policy are K. McRoberts, "Language Policy," in D.P. Shugarman and R. Whitaker, eds., *Federalism and Political Community: Essays in Honour of Donald Smiley* (Peterborough, Ont.: Broadview Press, 1989); and C. Taylor, "Shared and Divergent Values," in R.L. Watts and D.M. Brown, eds., *Options for a New Canada* (Toronto: University of Toronto Press, 1991).

language, but it is so important that they are unwilling to trade away its collective control in exchange for other benefits. People may want better social services and the advantages of an economic union but are not prepared to accept these gains if they entail sacrifice of control over language.

Arguably, one of the reasons for the success of the British Empire relative to that of other European powers was that British colonial administrators better understood colonial preferences. From Quebec to India, the British introduced variations on the federal theme of divided jurisdiction; they controlled commercial policy, imposing free trade and uniform commercial law; the local colonial elite maintained collective political jurisdiction over language and culture.

The Argument from External Effects
(the Economics of Language)

Although nationalist movements place a very high priority on the exercise of political jurisdiction over language, if that were the only argument for provincial linguistic jurisdiction, it would be a weak one. It amounts to the morality of *realpolitik*: choosing constitutional principles based on the preferences of the strongest or the most belligerent. Civil libertarians can always object to any exercise of collective political power over language because it necessarily imposes costs on those who want to live, work, and educate their children in some language other than that being promoted. A firm moral argument for designation of a provincial linguistic jurisdiction must address this critique from civil liberties.

The response rests on the external effects individual linguistic choices have on others. These effects are sufficiently important to weaken — although not to eliminate — the claim of adversely affected groups for linguistic freedom of choice. To treat language thus is to engage in moral evasion: to avoid a painful, but necessary political choice over which language will predominate in any political jurisdiction. Except in special instances, wherever a free linguistic market operates in which members of a "minor" linguistic group engage extensively with members of a "major" linguistic group, the "minor" language gives way intergenerationally to the "major" language and in the long run becomes residual.

The ability to speak and read a language is a kind of capital good. Like any other, it is costly — in terms of time and effort — to acquire; once the investment is made, it yields benefits. The first benefit is access to artifacts recorded in that language. A small number of people continue to learn ancient Greek in order to appreciate the plays of Euripides or to study the work of early Christian writers in the original. The second and most important benefit is the ability to communicate with others who also know the language. The third, an extension of the second, is the ability to participate, both as producer and consumer, in the market for new "cultural products" — from rock concerts to high-brow literary novels — using the particular language.

The second benefit entails an important external effect. Additional speakers of a language create a communication benefit not only for themselves but also for those who already have acquired the language; conversely, a decrease in the numbers of speakers lowers the communication benefit to those who acquired the language earlier. Consider the controversial case of allophone immigrants to Montreal. By learning French, immigrants gain the ability to communicate with their immediate francophone neighbors. But typical immigrants have weak attachments to their initial North American community; they realistically contemplate further migration within Canada, if not within all of North America. Since francophones comprise a small minority of North Americans, assimilation to English dramatically increases the ease of communication with the majority. In summary, the communication benefit of a language increases with the number speaking it. The costs of learning French or English are similar. Therefore it is understandable that most allophone immigrants, given freedom in choice of language, expected to maximize their net benefits by investing in the learning of English, not French. Prior to Quebec's recent language laws, an overwhelming majority did just that (see Appendix A, Table A-5). But if the proportion speaking French in Montreal diminishes, the benefit to francophones from their language is reduced.

We come to the third benefit, participation in the market for cultural products. Many such products demonstrate scale economies — that is, the unit cost of production is higher in small markets than in large ones. Once a promoter has decided to invest in a Richard Desjardins concert, for example, the cost of one more person in the audience is essentially zero. But without a large francophone population from which to draw, the promoter will not be able to lower the average fixed cost sufficiently to attract an audience at a price permitting a profit. The same argument applies to the high-brow novel. There must be enough readers to amortize the publisher's fixed expenses at a reasonable cost per book.

Without using the economic jargon, Québécois have realized the importance of external effects and scale economies ever since the Seven Years' War. They have consistently perceived themselves to be analogous to the Swedes, Danes, or Flemish, members of a cultural-linguistic market enjoying — just enough — scale economies to produce a rich culture, but one not sufficiently dominant to permit linguistic free trade.

Advocates of linguistic free trade are *de facto* implying that elimination of a "minor" language in favor of a "major" one poses no serious moral problems. Thus, anglophones and allophones who oppose Quebec's limits on the use of English must be prepared to argue that it is morally acceptable if Montreal eventually becomes a majority anglophone city. But such a linguistic outcome clearly does pose a serious moral problem: it is intensely opposed by the majority of Quebec residents.

Defenders of a linguistic free market can reasonably retort with the following question: Is it not equally valid to pose the linguistic problem as the survival of English as a "minor" language within Quebec? In other words, by shifting context, both the francophone and the anglophone communities can make a logically identical claim for government policy that advances their respective linguistic survival. Since the argument of both communities is identical, is it not arbitrary to choose one over the other?

When faced with this line of argument, we must ask what basis there is for choosing between French and English in Quebec or, in general, between the conflicting claims of members of different linguistic communities? If we are truly faced with the stark choice between the survival of either the anglophone or the francophone community in Quebec, the latter undeniably has the stronger claim for three reasons. The first is the idea of the constitution as a social contract. Interpretation of the BNA Act is a complex historical and legal exercise, but it is clear that by creating a federation, as opposed to a unitary state, all the Fathers of Confederation accepted — some willingly, some begrudgingly — something of the contemporary Québécois' claim that they constituted a "distinct society" relative to the other British North American colonies and that, via the Quebec National Assembly, they could advance their collective interests. At the time, denominational schools controlled by the Roman Catholic Church played the leading role in protecting the French language, and it is to be noted that the BNA Act explicitly made education a matter of provincial jurisdiction (section 93).

A second reason is simply utilitarian. Québécois constitute the majority within Quebec, and fewer will face linguistic losses with a policy that favors French than under an alternative — such as linguistic free trade — that favors English. (The implicit assumption here is that people have legitimate preferences with respect to the impact of the linguistic environment not only on themselves, but also on their children and future generations.)

A third reason is that the francophone majority of Quebec can give as credible a guarantee of minority linguistic rights as can any other linguistic majority. To emphasize the fundamental linguistic dilemma, I have posed the constitutional choice as one between irreconcilable principles. In practice, there is no need for victory to be total. Provided the Québécois majority retain unambiguously a general political power to legislate in this domain, it is reasonable to entrench a set of minority linguistic rights. Prior to the Quiet Revolution of the 1960s, such guarantees might have been suspect. For many years, the hierarchy of the Roman Catholic Church played a powerful role in Quebec that frustrated liberal intellectual discourse and marginalized linguistic and religious minorities; the worst offence was the passive acceptance of fascist antisemitic movements in the province during the 1930s.[16] But this circumstance no longer exists, and Quebec is now as tolerant and pluralist a society as any in the Western industrial world.[17]

The Argument from Discrimination

Knowledge of a society's "elite" language affords an individual an economic advantage independent of his or her qualifications. Such discrimination is not only unjust; it is inefficient. Less productive people secure promotion, and aggregate economic performance suffers. An extreme example is the disadvantage suffered by Russian speakers in their own country during the eighteenth and nineteenth century, when French was the language of choice of the aristocracy.

Although French was the elite language in nineteenth century Russia, it obviously was not in Quebec. Until this generation, English was Quebec's language of business. An important dimension of the

---

16 See G. Caldwell, "L'Antisémitisme au Québec," in P. Anctil and G. Caldwell, eds., *Juifs et Réalités Juives au Québec* (Québec: Institut québécois de recherche sur la culture, 1984).

17 This point needs to be emphasized. Mordecai Richler, in a much-publicized recent article, satirizes a number of administrative inanities arising from Quebec's language laws ("A Reporter at Large," *The New Yorker*, September 23, 1991). Such polemics are fair game. One aspect of Richler's article needs to be countered, however. The author concludes that Québécois are significantly more prone to antisemitism than other average Canadians. It is a charge he does not adequately support and, given the seriousness of the anti-Semitic blight in the twentieth century, one that should not be made lightly. The most damning piece of evidence he cites is a poll in which 84 percent of Québécois thought Jews were "pushy" (*"arriviste"*), as opposed to a national average of 40 percent. There exist important doubts about the methodology of this poll and additional evidence, none of it very conclusive, to suggest that antisemitism may actually be a more serious problem elsewhere in Canada. See P. Anctil, "Québec antisémite? Non coupable!" *L'Actualité*, December 1, 1991.

Quebec government's promotion of French has been the *francisation* of major firms, requiring them to operate in French. Typically, multinational firms, accustomed to doing business in many languages, have adapted to these regulations more readily than anglo-Canadian firms. Doubtless *francisation* has generated inefficiencies by, for example, accelerating emigration of some anglophone professionals, but it has probably contributed to the overall productivity of the Quebec economy by reducing a source of discrimination against francophones. Using 1971 data, Shapiro and Stelcner found significant evidence of discrimination in earnings: unilingual francophone males, for example, earned 19 percent less than comparably qualified unilingual anglophones. By 1981, that gap had fallen to 5 percent.[18]

As with all cases of positive discrimination, one must define the limits of redress. The sins of previous generations of the elite do not justify a regime of retribution once balance has been restored. One healthy recognition of limits is the current debate, led largely by Québécois, about the underrepresentation of anglophones in the Quebec public service and the need to increase their share.

Tactical Considerations: The Pepin-Robarts Report or the Beige Paper?

The election of the Parti Québécois government in 1976 prompted creation of the federal Task Force on Canadian Unity jointly chaired by Jean-Luc Pepin and John Robarts. Their 1979 report, academic in tone and clearly imbued with the Queen's University tradition of respect for classic federalism and desire for precision in the division of powers, recommended equality of status for French and English within the federal jurisdiction and the right of each province to declare an official language or languages within its jurisdiction, subject to a set of minority rights (see Appendix B).

---

18 D.M. Shapiro and M. Stelcner, "Earnings Disparities among Linguistic Groups in Quebec, 1970–1980," *Canadian Public Policy* 13 (1987): 97–104. The study uses 1971 and 1981 census data.

On the appropriate role of the Quebec government, the Pepin-Robarts Report concluded:

> We support the efforts of the Quebec provincial government and of the people of Quebec to ensure the predominance of the French language and culture in that province. We believe that the people of Quebec must feel as confident and secure in the present and future potential of their language and culture as do the people of Ontario and the other English-speaking provinces. There can be nothing more damaging, in our view, to the cause of Canadian unity than the rejection of these aspirations of francophone Québécois by English-speaking Canadians. We believe that present constitutional arrangements which allow the provinces to adopt those laws and regulations which they deem suitable are appropriate to the present and emerging Canadian social context.[19]

The following year, the Quebec Liberal Party, then led by Claude Ryan, came to similar conclusions in a report that came to be called the Beige Paper (for the color of its cover), the result of what is by far the most ambitious constitutional analysis of any Canadian political party in opposition (see Appendix B). It was the Beige Paper that introduced the term "distinct society" into the contemporary debate.

Quebec — A distinct society
...In effect, Quebec forms within the Canadian federation a society which is distinct in terms of its languages, its culture, its institutions and its way of life. Quebec is also the home of a large Anglophone community and numerous ethnic groups, concentrated mainly in Montreal. These communities and their institutions make up an essential dimension of Quebec life. But in general, Quebec sees itself and expresses itself as a society which is French, in language and in spirit. Within the Canadian political family, Quebec society has all the characteristics of a distinct national community.[20]

---

19 Canada, Task Force on Canadian Unity, p. 51.

20 Quebec Liberal Party, Constitutional Committee *A New Canadian Federation* (Quebec, 1980), pp. 12–13.

Prime Minister Pierre Trudeau, whose own intellectual position had long been critical of nationalist tendencies toward "tribalism," was hostile to the principle of provincial linguistic jurisdiction advanced by both reports. Upon defeating the Parti Québécois in the 1980 referendum, he oversaw patriation of the Constitution with the Charter of Rights and Freedoms, a document obviously inspired by the principle of free individual choice between French and English. It referred to English and French as the "official languages of Canada" [section 16(1)] but made no mention of any special role for the Quebec government in promoting French within its borders. Some of its clauses explicitly overrode provisions of Quebec's Bill 101; others were sufficiently ambiguous that the Supreme Court might be able to further erode Quebec linguistic jurisdiction — as, indeed, transpired in the language of signs case.

Although the 1982 patriation package had the legitimacy of support by the Liberal MPs from Quebec (74 of the total Quebec caucus of 75), those votes reflected more the strength of party discipline than the nature of Quebec society. In the Quebec National Assembly, a resolution rejecting the package was supported by the Parti Québécois government plus a majority of the opposition Liberal members.

The federal Conservative government of Brian Mulroney and the Quebec Liberal government of Robert Bourassa were subsequently elected, in part, on a commitment to undo the constitutional polarization generated by Trudeau's patriation package. The heart of their joint approach was the Meech Lake Accord, a constitutional amendment that would have introduced the concept of Quebec as a distinct society into the Constitution (see Appendix B). Subsection 2(3) of the amendment would have afforded Quebec a limited special status to "preserve and promote the distinct identity of Quebec," but subsection 2(2) affirmed the responsibility of all provinces, including Quebec, to preserve the bilingual status quo of the country, and subsection 2(4) stated that the distinct society clause would give no province new powers over language or any other matter.

Quebec Liberal Party leaders, who were imbued with the Beige Paper analysis, claimed the distinct society clause would give the government of Quebec broad powers to pursue autonomous policies, economic and social as well as linguistic. Opponents of the accord attacked it from all sides. Ardent Québécois nationalists emphasized its qualifiers and called it a fig leaf to mask Bourassa's naked constitutional defeat. Supporters of official bilingualism and the Charter viewed the distinct society clause as a Trojan horse smuggled into the constitutional fortress created by Trudeau's patriation exercise: it could potentially allow Quebec to disregard the spirit of the Charter at will, and it would violate the principle of symmetry among provinces. In ROC, those ill disposed to Québécois influence in federal politics — most made few distinctions between Trudeau and Mulroney — resented what they took to be any constitutional statement that Québécois were more "distinct" than other communities within the country.

Probably the most reasonable conclusion about the distinct society clause is that it would have provided Quebec with a basis for defending its linguistic policies before the courts. But since we do not know the tradition of judicial interpretation that would have arisen, we cannot know the substantive meaning of the section. In retrospect, we can see that the Meech Lake Accord was an attempt to resolve the conflict over appropriate linguistic principles by resorting to ambiguity. Much of the political attraction of the term "distinct society" to the accord's authors was that it avoided the painful exercise of delineating federal and provincial powers with some precision.

The federal constitutional proposals of September 1991 reintroduced a distinct society clause (see Appendix B). The new version, now located within the Charter as opposed to the body of the *Constitution Act*, is restricted to being a basis for interpretation of the Charter. Furthermore, "distinct society" is rendered somewhat less vague by the specification that it refers to Quebec's language, "unique culture," and civil law tradition. The qualifying subsections 2(2) and 2(4) of the Meech Lake version disappear, but, of course, section 31 of the Charter, which is the equivalent of subsection 2(4) remains.[21]

---

21 Section 31 of the Charter reads: "Nothing in this Charter extends the legislative powers of any body or authority."

If a majority of Canadians in ROC come to accept a version of the distinct society clause and if Québécois are satisfied that it adequately entrenches their collective powers over language and culture, then we should go with it. There is, after all, a case for constitutional ambiguity. (Ambiguity in the drafting of particular clauses in the BNA Act was necessary to achieve acceptance of Confederation by the various elites within the British North American colonies.)

The polls cited at the beginning of this essay imply, however, that Canadians are currently not in a mood to tolerate ambiguity, with the implicit understanding that judges sort matters out later. They suggest that nonfrancophones in ROC may balk at any version of "distinct society." Some analysts have attempted to place a more optimistic "spin" on the poll results cited earlier by adding together those ROC respondents in favor of a distinct society clause and the "soft" opponents — those who, while opposing the clause, would accept it as a final concession to get a deal. This exercise generates a slim majority — 53 or 56 percent[22] — within ROC willing to accept Quebec as a distinct society.

Personally, I am not reassured by this cobbled-together, slim majority on behalf of the distinct society clause. It may suffice; it may not.

Any constitutional agreement that reconciles the country and preserves the federation must, I am convinced, contain provisions that clearly satisfy the linguistic concerns of Québécois. In summary:

1. Any distinct society clause must clearly empower the Quebec government to pursue language policies that favor French over English.

---

22 The arithmetic is as follows. Using the *Globe and Mail* data: 53 percent, which is the 28 percent of ROC respondents in favor of the clause plus 25 percent in ROC who oppose it but "would accept the distinct society clause as a compromise to keep Quebec from separating." Using the *Maclean's* data: 56 percent, which is the sum of the 28 percent of ROC respondents in favor plus the 28 percent who oppose it but would "be prepared to see distinct society kept in the proposals if it is the only way to get a final agreement."

Provided the agreement contained other provisions that satis-factorily address the concerns of regions and interest groups outside Quebec, most premiers in ROC would probably be prepared to sell a distinct society clause to their skeptical electorates. These politi-cians are, however, acutely conscious of the extent of popular oppo-sition in ROC to the idea of Quebec as a distinct society and may be tempted to qualify the clause to a point at which it loses all meaning within Quebec or to remain neutral and fail to do battle with those who oppose its inclusion in the Constitution.

Relative to the Meech Lake version, the September 1991 federal proposal was already more qualified. The former stipulated that the entire Constitution should be interpreted in a manner that enabled the Quebec government "to preserve and promote the distinct iden-tity of Quebec"; the latter applied uniquely to interpretations of the Charter. The most recently proposed version — that of the Beaudoin-Dobbie parliamentary committee — was further qualified. Not only does this latest version apply solely to interpretations of the Charter, it imposes a more ambitious obligation on all governments, includ-ing Quebec's, toward official language minorities. In both the Meech Lake and the September 1991 federal versions, constitutional inter-pretation was to be based on their "preservation." The Beaudoin-Dobbie version requires an interpretation based on their "vitality and development...throughout Canada."

Might the courts interpret the "vitality and development" of Quebec anglophones to be sufficient grounds to strike down once again aspects of Quebec legislation restricting the use of English? At this point, any answer is speculative. Obviously, the authors of this latest version believed that earlier versions allowed the Quebec government too much latitude. By further qualifying the clause, however, they have endangered the primary purpose of any distinct society clause: to give a secure constitutional standing to Quebec's language regime.

2.   As an alternative to the distinct society clause — as a backup in case of need — we should resurrect for consideration the more explicit

division of language jurisdiction recommended by the Pepin-Robarts Report.

An explicit provision of a provincial jurisdiction over language would, polls suggest, satisfy the majority of Québécois. It would also probably be more acceptable in ROC than the distinct society approach. No longer would constitutional reform require ROC residents to accept that Quebec is a society "more distinct" than theirs. It is important to emphasize here that the designation of an explicit provincial domain of language jurisdiction would in no way preclude Ottawa from pursuing bilingual policies within its jurisdiction. Indeed, both the Pepin-Robarts Report and the Beige Paper explicitly advocated constitutional entrenchment of a set of bilingual rights within federal jurisdiction.

If we are to prevent the courts from triggering a future sign law fiasco, the courts must not interpret the Charter right to freedom of expression so broadly. It is probably appropriate to amend this section to state explicitly that government regulation of commercial use of language is permissible.

3.   Given the extent of linguistic mistrust present, minority linguistic rights presumably should be within the Constitution and not, as proposed by Pepin-Robarts, in the form of provincial statutes.

The four basic rights that linguistic minorities should expect from their provincial government are:

* the right of official language minorities to have their children educated in that language where numbers warrant;[23]
* the right of official language minorities to receive basic provincial government services, including but not limited to health care and social services, in their language where numbers warrant;
* the right of official language minorities to conduct major criminal court proceedings in their language; and

23 Variations exist in the scope of definition of this right — that the official language minority citizen must have received her instruction in the minority language within the province in question, within Canada, or — what would be an extension from the status quo — anywhere in the world.

- the right of allophone linguistic minorities to reasonable government support in preserving their linguistic heritage.

The unambiguous losers from constitutional entrenchment of provincial jurisdiction over language would be Pierre Trudeau and Jacques Parizeau. The former would face the explicit jettisoning of his constitutional theses on language and the symmetry of provinces. The latter would lose the most emotionally powerful argument for Quebec sovereignty: that ROC will never explicitly permit Québécois to exercise political power to preserve their language and culture.

Likely Outcomes

How would explicit provincial jurisdiction likely affect linguistic communities across the country?

Québécois

In the present context of constitutional ambiguity, Québécois are legitimately fearful that administrative flexibility creates irreversible precedents. They have shown consistently since the 1960s their intent to exercise jurisdiction over language within the province. They have obtained the benefits — and paid certain costs — of elevating French as the province's official language. An optimistic but nonetheless reasonable prognosis is that if their constitutional jurisdiction over language were secure — in other words, if ROC accepted the legitimacy of Quebec's language initiatives — Québécois would be more prepared to negotiate flexible language laws that would satisfy the province's anglophone and allophone minorities better than the present ones.

Anglophone and Allophone Minorities in Quebec

Quebec's anglophone and allophone minorities would have to accept *de jure* what now they accept *de facto*: that their linguistic communities will not receive provincial government support equal to that afforded to French, and that they will face certain linguistic constraints on use of English in the province. As just suggested, however, the actual linguistic regime might well improve for them. (A majority of Québécois probably now support the position that, although the Quebec government should have the jurisdiction to introduce legislation such as Bill 178, the actual law is too restrictive.)

Allophone Communities in ROC

Provincial governments in ROC would have constitutional sanction to design various language policies suited to the local linguistic distribution. These policies could range from official bilingualism in New Brunswick to better Ukrainian courses in Prairie schools to better services in Cantonese and Punjabi in British Columbia. Meanwhile, symbolic extensions of official bilingualism on behalf of francophone minorities would doubtless cease. (For example, the obligations on Western provincial governments to translate their statutes into French would probably be eliminated.) These symbolic policies have angered the anglophone majority and have probably had the unintended effect of limiting the willingness of provincial governments to support the preservation of the linguistic heritage of allophone communities.

Francophones in ROC

If linguistic jurisdiction within Quebec was settled, Ottawa would have less interest in attempting to use subsidies buttressing French in ROC to persuade Quebec francophones to accept official bilingualism. Thus, francophones in ROC might well be net losers. However, as the linguistic data indicate, it is only in the bilingual belts of eastern Ontario and northern New Brunswick that ROC francophones can reasonably expect to resist assimilation. If they concentrate on policy in these two provinces, they will no longer be pawns in the conflict over Quebec language policy or bear the resentment of allophones over "unfair privileges."

Conclusion

Despite recent constitutional convulsions, Canadians have created one of the most prosperous and tolerant states in the modern world. One of the key ingredients in this success has been the creative application of federalism. There is no guarantee that explicit decentralization of language policy will produce the results suggested by Eduard Shevardnadze, Marcel Côté, and Robert Stanfield. (Certainly, it did not suffice to prevent conflict in Georgia.) Nonetheless, actual federal policy since the 1960s — the pursuit of official bilingualism across the country, combined with a refusal to recognize Quebec as holding an important domain of jurisdiction over language — has undeniably been one of the principal causes of our continued constitutional paralysis.

In the pragmatic world of politics, the need is always to compare one policy against another, not against an ideal. On that basis, an explicit division of linguistic jurisdiction is superior to the alternative of linguistic free trade. That conclusion must not imply contempt for Trudeau's ideal of a country truly bilingual from coast to coast. Although it can never be realized to the extent he desired, we must preserve a significant bilingual minority across the country in order to avoid the threat of our two solitudes degenerating into René Lévesque's scorpions squabbling in a bottle.

Appendix A:
Summary Statistics on Language in Canada

Table A-1:   Distribution of Population in Regions of Canada, by Language Community

	Francophones	Anglophones	Allophones	Share of Canadian Population
	(percentage of population)			
By mother tongue				
Quebec				
1931	79.7	15.0	5.3	27.7
1951	82.5	13.8	3.7	29.0
1971	80.7	13.1	6.2	27.9
1986	82.9	10.3	6.8	25.8
Rest of Canada				
1931	7.2	73.1	19.7	72.3
1951	7.2	77.6	15.2	71.0
1971	6.0	78.4	15.6	72.1
1986	5.0	80.1	14.9	74.2
All Canada				
1931	27.3	57.0	15.7	
1951	29.0	59.1	11.9	
1971	26.9	60.1	13.0	
1986	25.1	62.1	12.8	
By language of use, 1986				
Quebec	82.8	12.3	4.9	
Rest of Canada	3.6	88.6	7.8	
All Canada	24.1	68.9	7.0	

Source: Marc Termote, "L'évolution démolinguistique du Québec et du Canada," in Quebec, Commission on the Political and Constitutional Future of Quebec [Bélanger-Campeau Commission], *Éléments d'analyse institutionnelle, juridique et démolinguistique pertinents à la révision du statut politique et constitutionnel du Québec* [Background papers], vol. 2 (Quebec, 1991).

Table A-2:   *Distribution of Population in Regions of Quebec, by Language Community*

	Francophones	Anglophones	Allophones	Share of Quebec Population
	(percentage of population)			
By *mother tongue*				
Montreal and Laval[a]				
1941	63.8	26.0	10.2	34.2
1971	63.2	22.6	14.2	36.3
1986	62.9	19.6	17.5	31.2
Suburban Montreal[b]				
1941	84.3	13.4	2.3	9.0
1971	82.7	14.6	2.7	14.8
1986	87.0	9.8	3.2	19.3
Rest of Quebec[c]				
1941	91.8	7.0	1.2	56.9
1971	93.2	5.5	1.3	48.9
1986	93.8	4.7	1.5	49.5
By *language of use*, 1986				
Montreal and Laval[a]	62.4	23.9	13.7	
Suburban Montreal[b]	86.8	11.1	2.1	
Rest of Quebec[c]	93.6	5.1	1.3	

[a] The Island of Montreal and Île Jésus.

[b] Comprising the following 16 census divisions surrounding the Island of Montreal and Île Jésus: Argenteuil, Beauharnois, Chambly, Châteauguay, Deux-Montagnes, Huntingdon, Iberville, Laprairie, L'Assomption, Napierville, Rouville, Saint-Jean, Soulanges, Terrebonne, Vaudreuil, and Verchères.

[c] Quebec minus the Greater Montreal area (comprising the Island of Montreal, Île Jésus, and the 16 surrounding census divisions noted above).

Source: Marc Termote, "L'évolution démolinguistique du Québec et du Canada," in Quebec, Commission on the Political and Constitutional Future of Quebec [Bélanger-Campeau Commission], *Éléments d'analyse institutionnelle, juridique et démolinguistique pertinents à la révision du statut politique et constitutionnel du Québec* [Background papers], vol. 2 (Quebec, 1991).

Table A-3: *Distribution of Population in Language Communities, by Regions of Canada*

	Quebec	Rest of Canada
	(percentage of language group)	
Mother tongue		
French		
1931	80.9	19.1
1971	84.0	16.0
1986	85.1	14.9
English		
1931	7.3	92.7
1971	6.1	93.9
1986	4.3	95.7
Other		
1931	9.4	90.6
1971	13.3	86.7
1986	13.7	86.3
Language of use, 1986		
French	88.8	11.2
English	4.6	95.4
Other	17.9	82.1

Source: Marc Termote, "L'évolution démolinguistique du Québec et du Canada," in Quebec, Commission on the Political and Constitutional Future of Quebec [Bélanger-Campeau Commission], *Éléments d'analyse institutionnelle, juridique et démolinguistique pertinents à la révision du statut politique et constitutionnel du Québec* [Background papers], vol. 2 (Quebec, 1991).

**Table A-4:   Linguistic Mobility of
Allophone Immigrants to Quebec, 1986**

	Adopted as Language of Use	
Date of Immigration	French	English
	(percentage of subgroup)	
Before 1966	8	26
1966–70	11	18
1971–75	12	13
1976–78	13	9
1979–81	10	6
1982–86	7	7

Note: the percentages listed refer to those declaring a *single* official language of use. Approximately 15 percent of each immigration subgroup, except the most recent, listed use of
both official languages.

Source: Marc Termote, "L'évolution démolinguistique du Québec et du Canada," in Quebec,
Commission on the Political and Constitutional Future of Quebec [Bélanger-Campeau
Commission], *Éléments d'analyse institutionnelle, juridique et démolinguistique pertinents à
la révision du statut politique et constitutionnel du Québec* [Background papers], vol. 2
(Quebec, 1991).

**Table A-5:   Knowledge of an Official
Language Not the Mother Tongue**

	English among Nonanglophones	French among Nonfrancophones
Quebec		
1931	33	28
1971	29	40
1986	33	62
Rest of Canada		
1931	79	1
1971	86	4
1986	89	6

Source: Marc Termote, "L'évolution démolinguistique du Québec et du Canada," in Quebec,
Commission on the Political and Constitutional Future of Quebec [Bélanger-Campeau
Commission], *Éléments d'analyse institutionnelle, juridique et démolinguistique pertinents à
la révision du statut politique et constitutionnel du Québec* [Background papers], vol. 2
(Quebec, 1991).

Appendix B:
Selected Constitutional Documents on Language

Report of the Task Force on Canadian Unity (Pepin-Robarts), Recommendations on Language, 1979

1. The principle of the equality of status, rights and privileges of the English and French languages for all purposes declared by the Parliament of Canada, within its sphere of jurisdiction, should be entrenched in the constitution.

   These purposes should include:
   (i) The equality of both official languages in the Parliament of Canada;
   (ii) the right of members of the public to obtain services from and communicate with the head offices of every department, agency or Crown corporation of the Government of Canada, the central administration in the National Capital Region, and all federal courts in Canada in either of the official languages. Elsewhere, members of the public should be able to obtain services from and communicate with the central administration in both official languages where there is significant demand, and to the extent that it is feasible to provide such services;
   (iii) the equality of both official languages as languages of work in the central administration in the National Capital Region, in all federal courts, and in the head offices of every department, agency or Crown corporation of the Government of Canada. Elsewhere, the usual language or languages of work in central institutions should be the language or languages of work normally used in the province in which the central institution is operating. This recommendation is subject to the previous recommendation concerning the languages of service;
   (iv) the right of any person to give evidence in the official language of his or her choice in any criminal matter;

    (v)   the right of every person to have access to radio and television services in both the French and English languages;

    (vi)   the availability in both official languages of all printed material intended for general public use.

2. Each provincial legislature should have the right to determine an official language or official languages for that province, within its sphere of jurisdiction.

3. Linguistic rights should be expressed in provincial statutes, which could include:

    (i)   the entitlement recognized in the statement of the provincial first ministers at Montreal in February 1978: "Each child of a French-speaking or English-speaking minority is entitled to an education in his or her language in the primary or secondary schools in each province, wherever numbers warrant." This right should also be accorded to children of either minority who change their province of residence.

    (ii)   the right of every person to receive essential health and social services in his or her principal language, be it French or English, wherever numbers warrant.

    (iii) the right of an accused in a criminal trial to be tried in his or her principal language, be it French or English, wherever it is feasible.

4. Should all provinces agree on these or any other linguistic rights, these rights should then be entrenched in the constitution.

5. The provinces should review existing methods and procedures for the teaching and learning of both French and English and make greater efforts to improve the availability and quality of instruction in these languages at all levels of education.

Report of the Quebec Liberal Party (the Beige Paper), Recommendations on Language, 1980

1. A Charter of Rights and Liberties should be enshrined in the constitution.

2. The Charter should protect the fundamental rights to life, freedom, physical integrity and privacy; it will also guarantee freedom of thought, of religion, of opinion, of speech, of association and freedom of the press, as well as the basic principles of non-discrimination;

3. The Charter would also enshrine legal rights including:
    (a) the right of equality before the law and to the protection of the law;
    (b) the right of every person to a public and impartial hearing by an independent tribunal;
    (c) the right of every person who is arrested or detained to be promptly informed of the reasons for his arrest or detention and to be promptly brought before a competent tribunal;
    (d) the right of protection from unreasonable seizures and searches.

4. The Charter should ensure the right of each Canadian to settle anywhere in Canada and to enjoy rights identical to those of the citizens of the province where he settles.

5. The constitution should recognize that French and English are the official languages of federal political institutions as well as of those bodies which fall within their jurisdiction.

6. The provinces should be empowered to legislate with respect to language, subject however to certain inviolate rights safeguarded by the constitutionally enshrined Charter of Rights and Liberties.

7. The constitution should extend to Ontario and New Brunswick those obligations already incumbent upon Quebec and Manitoba by virtue of sections 133 of the B.N.A. Act and 23 of the Manitoba Act.

8. The Charter should recognize the following language rights:

(a) the right of any French or English-speaking person as well as of any native person to be served by the federal government in their language, wherever the number of people seeking such services justifies it;

(b) the right of every French or English-speaking person and every native person to request primary and secondary level education for their children the province in which they reside in their mother tongue;

(c) the right of French-speaking, English-speaking and native communities whenever they constitute sufficiently large groups, to administer their own public educational institutions;

(d) the right of every person to have access to health and social services in their own language, be it French or English, where the number warrants it;

(e) the right of every French or English-speaking person as well as every native person to demand that a criminal or penal trial which exposes them to possible imprisonment be held in their mother tongue;

(f) the right of every French or English-speaking person to demand access in every region of the country to radio and television services in their mother tongue where the number of people seeking such services justifies it.

Charter of Rights and Freedoms, Sections on Language, 1982

Official Languages of Canada

Official languages of Canada

16. (1) English and French are the official languages of Canada and have equality of status and equal rights and privileges as to their use in all institutions of the Parliament and government of Canada.

Official languages of New Brunswick

(2) English and French are the official languages of New Brunswick and have equality of status and equal rights and privileges as to their use in all institutions of the legislature and government of New Brunswick.

Advancement of status and use

(3) Nothing in this Charter limits the authority of Parliament or a legislature to advance the equality of status or use of English and French.

Proceedings of Parliament

17. (1) Everyone has the right to use English or French in any debates and other proceedings of Parliament.

Proceedings of New Brunswick legislature

(2) Everyone has the right to use English or French in any debates or other proceedings of the legislature of New Brunswick.

Parliamentary statutes and records

18. (1) The statutes, records and journals of Parliament shall be printed and published in English and French and both language versions are equally authoritative.

New Brunswick statutes and records

(2) The statutes, records and journals of the legislature of New Brunswick shall be printed and published in English and French and both language versions are equally authoritative.

Proceedings in courts established by Parliament

19. (1) Either English or French may be used by any person in, or in any pleading in or process issuing from, any court established by Parliament.

(2) Either English or French may be used by any person in, or in any pleading in or process issuing from, any court of New Brunswick.

Communications by public with federal institutions

20. (1) Any member of the public in Canada has the right to communicate with, and to receive available services from, any head or central office of an institution of the Parliament or government of Canada in English or French, and has the same right with respect to any other office of any such institution where

(a) there is a significant demand for communications with and services from that office in such language; or

(b) due to the nature of the office, it is reasonable that communications with and services from that office be available in both English and French.

Communications by public with New Brunswick institutions

(2) Any member of the public in New Brunswick has the right to communicate with, and to receive available services from, any office of an institution of the legislature or government of New Brunswick in English or French.

Communications by public with New Brunswick institutions

(2) Any member of the public in New Brunswick has the right to communicate with, and to receive available services from, any office of an institution of the legislature or government of New Brunswick in English or French.

Continuation of existing constitutional provisions

21. Nothing in sections 16 to 20 abrogates or derogates from any right, privilege or obligation with respect to the English and French languages, or either of them, that exists or is continued by virtue of any other provision of the Constitution of Canada.

Rights and privileges preserved

22. Nothing in sections 16 to 20 abrogates or derogates from any legal or customary right or privilege acquired or enjoyed either before or after the coming into force of this Charter with respect to any language that is not English or French.

Minority Language Educational Rights

Language of
instruction

23. (1) Citizens of Canada

(a) whose first language learned and still understood is that of the English or French linguistic minority population of the province in which they reside, or

(b) who have received their primary school instruction in Canada in English or French and reside in a province where the language in which they received that instruction is the language of the English or French linguistic minority population of the province,

have the right to have their children receive primary and secondary school instruction in that language in that province.

Continuity
of language
instruction

(2) Citizens of Canada of whom any child has received or is receiving primary or secondary school instruction in English or French in Canada, have the right to have all their children receive primary and secondary school instruction in the same language.

Application
where numbers
warrant

(3) The right of citizens of Canada under subsections (1) and (2) to have their children receive primary and secondary school instruction in the language of the English or French linguistic minority population of a province

(a) applies wherever in the province the number of children of citizens who have such a right is sufficient to warrant the provision to them out of public funds of minority language instruction; and

(b) includes, where the number of those children so warrants, the right to have them receive that instruction in minority language educational facilities provided out of public funds.

Meech Lake Accord, "Distinct Society" Clause, 1987

1. The *Constitution Act, 1867* is amended by adding thereto, immediately after section 1 thereof, the following section:

Interpretation

2. (1) The Constitution of Canada shall be interpreted in a manner consistent with

(a) the recognition that the existence of French-speaking Canadians, centred in Quebec but also present elsewhere in Canada, and English-speaking Canadians, concentrated outside Quebec but also present in Quebec, constitutes a fundamental characteristic of Canada; and

(b) the recognition that Quebec constitutes within Canada a distinct society.

Role of Parliament and legislatures

(2) The role of the Parliament of Canada and the provincial legislatures to preserve the fundamental characteristics of Canada referred to in paragraph (1)(a) is affirmed.

Role of legislature and Government of Quebec

(3) The role of the legislature and Government of Quebec to preserve and promote the distinct identity of Quebec referred to in paragraph (1)(b) is affirmed.

Rights of legislatures and governments

(4) Nothing in this section derogates from the powers, rights or privileges of Parliament or the Government of Canada, or of the legislatures or governments of the provinces, including any powers, rights or privileges relating to language.

Federal Constitutional Proposals, "Distinct Society" Clause, September 1991

25.1 (1) This Charter shall be interpreted in a manner consistent with

(a) the preservation and promotion of Quebec as a distinct society within Canada; and

(b) the preservation of the existence of French-speaking Canadians, primarily located in Quebec but also present throughout Canada, and English-speaking Canadians, primarily located outside Quebec but also present in Quebec.

(2) For the purposes of subsection (1), "distinct society", in relation to Quebec, includes

(a) a French-speaking majority;

(b) a unique culture; and

(c) a civil law tradition.

Report of the Special Joint Committee on a Renewed Canada (Beaudoin-Dobbie Committee), "Distinct Society" Clause, February 1992

25.1 (1) This Charter shall be interpreted in a manner consistent with

(a) the preservation and promotion of Quebec as a distinct society within Canada; and

(b) the vitality and development of the language and culture of French-speaking and English-speaking minority communities throughout Canada.

(2) For the purposes of subsection (1), "distinct society", in relation to Quebec, includes

(a) a French-speaking majority;

(b) a unique culture; and

(c) a civil law tradition.

A Comment

Yvon Fontaine

John Richards' thesis — a territorial approach as the basis for Canada's linguistic regime — is well known. As long ago as 1967, the Royal Commission on Bilingualism and Biculturalism, co-chaired by A. Davidson Dunton and André Laurendeau, endorsed a system based on the recognition in law and in practice of two official languages not only in areas where large communities of French- and English-speaking people were present, but also where one of the two languages was spoken by a minority group. Many people argued then that such an approach was inappropriate. Since that time, federally funded commissions, such as the Task Force on Canadian Unity (the Pepin-Robarts Task Force) — which reported ten years after the enactment of the *Official Languages Act* in 1969 — and more recently the Citizens' Forum on Canada's Future (the Spicer Commission), as well as many respected academics, have argued that Canada should reassess the foundations of its linguistic regime.

Their argument is simple: the present system has failed to create a bilingual country from coast to coast. Not only has current language policy failed to halt the assimilation of French-speaking communities outside Quebec — and even if it had, their numbers do not warrant such a generous policy — but it has also failed to solve tensions between Quebec and the rest of Canada.

Richards suggests that bilingualism is a reality only because of government subsidies. He serves up a potpourri of statistics to advance his thesis that, even with government support, the French fact outside Quebec is a myth and that francophones outside that province are losing the battle. He also refers to opinion polls that suggest that "the majority of anglophones and allophones clearly accept official bilingualism within the federal jurisdiction, but they simultaneously believe it has been extended too far at the behest of francophones."

Richards favors numbers, but what about history, fairness, and respect of Canada's social contract? Statistics can always be called on to prove a thesis. Volumes of statistics could be produced to prove the success of both the present linguistic regime and the linguistic policies of the past 25 years.

A *Globe and Mail*/CBC poll published in April 1991 indicated that 60 percent of anglophones and 75 percent of francophones — including French-speaking québécois — preferred a bilingual country from coast to coast to a territorial solution. The poll also reported that 60 percent of anglophones and 88 percent of francophones believed that official language minorities were entitled to receive public services in their own language. The number of Canadians who speak both languages has increased significantly in the past decade; French is being spoken by more and more Canadians outside Quebec.

Canada's linguistic regime has not stopped the rate of assimilation of the French-speaking population outside Quebec, but the situation is looking brighter. Things are not falling apart, they are falling in place. Section 23 of the Charter of Rights and Freedoms guarantees the linguistic minority population the right to receive primary and secondary school instruction in its own language in minority language educational facilities. Part VII of the 1988 *Official Languages Act* deals with the advancement of English and French. More specifically, section 41 states clearly that the federal government is committed to enhancing the vitality of the English and French linguistic minority communities and to supporting their development. These measures reflect the shift in the nature of linguistic rights in this country, and they establish a linguistic regime that will help to reverse the trend of assimilation of francophones outside Quebec. Ten years after the entrenchment of section 23 in the Charter, francophones are just beginning to reap the benefits. This, coupled with a generous application of the *Official Languages Act* by the federal government, will help linguistic minorities build distinct institutions that, in turn, will counter assimilation.

This being said, I do not believe we should rely solely or even primarily on numbers to determine the nature and the scope of Canada's linguistic regime. History, reasonable expectations, and fairness are important elements in the discussion.

Francophones, whether they live in Quebec or in other parts of Canada, have contributed immensely to the development of this land. They have left their mark in every province, from Maillardville, British Columbia to Port-aux-Basques, Newfoundland, from Gravelbourg, Saskatchewan to l'Ile Madame, Nova Scotia, from St-Paul, Alberta to Paquetville, New Brunswick, from St-Norbert, Manitoba to Lafontaine, Ontario. These names remind us that francophones were major players in the establishment of Canada. At the same time, however, one should not forget the essential role that the English-speaking community played in Quebec. Anglophones were a major force in the economic development of Montreal, for example, which in turn was an essential factor in the establishment of institutions such as McGill University.

In the middle of the nineteenth century, francophones represented a majority of the population of what is now British Columbia. Daniel Lavoie's song "jour the plaine" is a clear expression of how deeply the francophone communities on the Prairies are attached to that land. Francophones participated in a major way in the opening up of Northern Ontario. Acadians have been present in the Maritimes for 390 years — reason enough to argue their right to equal partnership with anglophones and aboriginal peoples in Canada.

Those are the historical realities that led to the creation of a Canadian federalism based on the principle of two major linguistic communities, and that greatly influenced the recommendations of the Laurendeau-Dunton Commission 25 years ago. Since then, the Commission's recommendations have been used to set forth language policies based on the principle of personality, not territoriality.

When examining the principle of territoriality — that is, a French Quebec and an English Canada — the members of the Laurendeau-

Dunton Commission observed that this concept would lead institutions to adopt unilingualism as a general rule and regard bilingualism as an exception when other means proved unavailable. Such rules of conduct, according to the commissioners, would be unjust and mean, and would ignore Canada's solidly embedded historical and social realities. This led them to favor a language rights system that respected both linguistic communities across Canada. An important role was given to the federal government, and several of the Commission's recommendations imposed certain obligations on provincial governments. The federal government and New Brunswick responded diligently to the Commission's recommendations by enacting laws making French and English official languages in their jurisdictions. Another 20 years would elapse before Ontario would pass Bill 8, which provides for French-language services to the franco-Ontarian community.

Had it not been for the leadership of the federal government, the conclusions of the Laurendeau-Dunton Commission would have been ignored and forgotten. Continuing federal involvement is of primary importance if we are to have a country that is proud of its two official languages and that respects the people of either linguistic community. If the federal government did not constantly push the issue, provincial governments would refuse to respect their legal and constitutional obligations in the area of language, just as they have in the past. Francophones remember only too well Manitoba's *School Act of 1891*, Ontario's Regulation 17 in 1913 forbidding French-language instruction in the schools, Manitoba's refusal to comply with section 23 of *The Manitoba Act, 1870* until the Supreme Court of Canada declared all of its laws unconstitutional in 1985, and the failure of Saskatchewan and Alberta to respect their constitutional obligations toward their francophone minorities after becoming provinces. More recently, some provinces have been reluctant to implement section 23 of the Charter of Rights and Freedoms, even after parents had fought them successfully in the Supreme Court of Canada.

The case for provincial jurisdiction over language, as Richards advocates, goes against basic principles of Canada's Constitution.

Both the federal government and the provinces are sovereign in their own spheres of jurisdiction. Accordingly, when exercising their powers over their respective jurisdictions, their right to oversee the linguistic dimension, attached to those powers, should not be tampered with. In addition, why should the federal government be denied the promotion of the linguistic duality of this country, when it actively promotes multiculturalism? Linguistic duality is both a fundamental characteristic of Canada and a national asset. It is the responsibility of all levels of government to make certain that it remains a vital part of our heritage.

I will concede that Richards is suggesting that certain basic rights of linguistic minorities be recognized, but the rights he mentions are limited in their scope. Moreover, certain dangers are inherent in such an approach. Entrenching those rights, which would create obligations exclusively on the part of the provinces, is much too risky, for reasons just discussed.

What is desperately needed is constitutional recognition of the existence of two major linguistic collectivities in this country, both being present throughout Canada, with governments' express commitment to contribute to the vitality and the development of the linguistic minority communities where needed. This does not mean additional constitutional rights to protect the French and English languages. To recognize Quebec's distinctiveness, without at the same time recognizing Canada's linguistic duality, is to deny the history of this country.

I was most impressed by the recommendations of the Special Joint Committee on a Renewed Canada (the Beaudoin-Dobbie Committee), which show a strong commitment to Canada's linguistic duality. In particular, the Committee proposes that the Charter of Rights and Freedoms be interpreted in a manner consistent with "the vitality and development of the language and culture of French-speaking and English-speaking minority communities throughout Canada" — a commitment also affirmed in a proposed section 2 to the Constitution, the so-called Canada Clause. The Committee also suggests that "double majority" voting along linguistic lines — as opposed to provincial boundaries — be introduced in the Senate on matters affecting the language or culture of French-speaking communities.

A recent study for the Fédération des communautés franco-phones et acadienne recommends a renewed linguistic regime that would center around a community development approach, rather than the creation of a variety of new rights.[1] Efforts would focus on the development of cultural, social, and economic spaces, which would help strengthen the communities. While this approach does not require new government programs to succeed, it does require governments to take into account Canada's linguistic duality in all program delivery.

For francophones, Richards' proposal, while it would guarantee certain basic linguistic rights, is simply not enough. It does not allow for the preservation and development of the French language and culture in this country. Francophones need a sense of belonging to a community in which their language and culture are present and vital.

---

1 Fédération des communautés francophones et acadienne du Canada, *Project 2000: For a Francophone Space* (Ottawa, 1992).

English and Anglophones in Quebec:
An Economic Perspective

François Vaillancourt

The purpose of this paper is to examine from an economic perspective the role of English and of anglophones in Quebec, be it independent or not. This topic is of interest since Quebec pursues explicit language policies that, along with other policies, have an impact on both English and anglophones and since changes in the constitutional status of Quebec would be likely to affect the place of English and anglophones in Quebec. The paper is divided into two sections. The first sets out the status of English and anglophones relative to French and francophones as well as some aspects of the makeup of Quebec's three language communities (francophone, anglophone, and allophone), including migration patterns. This information provides background for the second half of the paper, in which I put forward an analytical framework and then use it to recommend appropriate language policies for Quebec.

I wish to thank the C.D. Howe Institute for having asked me to prepare this paper, John Parisella for inviting me to present some of these ideas at a 1982 Alliance Quebec roundtable, participants at a Centre de recherche et développement en écono-mique (CRDE) workshop in July 1991, André Blais and André Raynauld for comments on a first draft, and David Brown and Daniel Schwanen of the C.D. Howe Institute and John McCallum of McGill University for comments on the penultimate version.

Part of the work on this paper was done while I was a resident associate at the Institute for Policy Analysis, University of Toronto and a visiting fellow at the Federalism Research Centre, Australian National University, Canberra.

Quebec's Population

This section of the paper is divided into two parts. The first examines the status of anglophones and English relative to francophones and French in the fields of education and work, as well as some aspects of the makeup of the anglophone and francophone communities in Quebec. Information on allophones — individuals whose mother tongue is a language other than English or French — is also presented when data were available and relevant. This information helps to establish the socioeconomic context in which the policies I propose would be introduced.

The second part examines migration, which has been one response by anglophones to changes in their status in Quebec.

For convenience, an appendix at the end of the paper gathers together the tables on which this section is based.

Status and Makeup of Quebec's Language Groups

Status

The socioeconomic status of francophones and French has been improving in Quebec since 1970, as evidenced by data on the language of schooling, the language of work, the value of French in the workplace, and the control by language groups of the economy.

The percentage of anglophone and allophone students who attended French-language primary and secondary schools, as well as CEGEPs (community colleges), increased steadily in the 1980s (Tables A-1 and A-2). One reason was legal constraints: the French schooling requirements of Bill 101 as applied to immigrants are a key determinant of allophones' language of schooling at the elementary and secondary levels. At the CEGEP level, the matter is one of choice; the increase in French-language CEGEP schooling is not surprising, however, since the language of schooling at the high school level is an important determinant of the language of CEGEP studies.[1]

In the workplace, the use of French has also been much more common in recent years (Table A-3), and skill in the language is increasingly required for various types of employment (for some evidence, see Table A-4).

Simultaneously, there has been an increase for individual workers in the economic value of using French. One can examine the value of a language in the labor market roughly by examining the mean earnings of various language groups or more carefully by calculating the same figures while controlling for other determinants of earnings — education, experience, and weeks worked. Both methods show that the relative returns to French have been improving in Quebec (see Tables A-5 and A-6). The results of the latter method are particularly relevant since they show a reversal for males in the Quebec market from 1970, when English brought larger returns than French, to 1985, when French brought larger returns than English.

Finally, francophones have increased their control over the Quebec economy as evidenced by the rise in the percentage of managers who are francophones (see Table A-7) and by increases in the francophone ownership of various sectors (see Table A-8).

All these factors clearly indicate that the socioeconomic status of francophones and French has been improving in Quebec since 1970, a fact that has implications for the language policies discussed later in this paper.

Makeup

Quebec's population in 1986 was made up of 82.9 percent francophones, 10.3 percent anglophones, and 6.8 percent allophones.[2]

---

1 Conseil de la langue française, *Indicateurs de la situation linguistique au Quebec* (Quebec: CLF, 1991), p. 39.

2 Ibid., p. 3. Notice that these figures differ slightly from those I report in Table A-9; contrary to the data reported there, the CLF percentages include children, allophones who know neither French nor English, and individuals in the census category of having both French and English as mother tongues.

Whether they know French, English, or both tends to vary with their age, their place of origin, and in some cases, where they live in Quebec.

Among adults, bilingualism is more prevalent among younger people than older ones; the difference is particularly notable among anglophones (see Table A-9). Also, adult anglophones who have a knowledge of French are much more likely to be Quebec-born than those who do not (see Table A-10).

As for place of residence in Quebec, anglophones and allophones are more concentrated in the Montreal area than francophones (see Table A-11). There is no difference in the location of unilingual and bilingual anglophones, which is surprising since one would expect anglophones from outside Quebec to be more likely both to be unilingual and to reside in Montreal, which has much more head-office employment than other places in Quebec. Such a pattern holds for younger, but not older, unilingual anglophones, who are often Quebec-born.

Mobility

Because of institutional constraints on immigration, the migration flows between Quebec and "the Rest of Canada" (ROC) are much more important than international migration flows for the anglophone community. The most recent evidence on migration by language groups shows much higher migration out of Quebec by anglophones than by francophones over the 1966–86 period and, since 1976, higher migration into Quebec in absolute numbers by francophones (see Table A-12).

This differentiated migration has consequences for the number of anglophones in Quebec. Using 1981 census data, Termote and Gauvreau find that the probability of survival — that is, of living to a given age in Quebec — differs markedly by language group (see Table A-13).[3] For example, an anglophone born in Quebec has only a 19 percent probability of surviving there at age 35, while a franco-

---

3 M. Termote and D. Gauvreau, *La situation démolinguistique au Quebec* (Quebec: Conseil de la langue française, 1988).

phone has a 91 percent probability. Survival depends, of course, on both mortality and mobility rates, but the anglophone-francophone difference here results almost entirely from mobility.

Using 1986 census data and differentiating between unilinguals and bilinguals, I obtain similar results (see Table A-14). Specifically, for Quebec-born individuals, I find:

- The loss of francophones, especially unilingual ones, is very small compared to that of anglophones.
- The loss of anglophones increases and then decreases with age, peaking with the 30- to 34-year-old cohort.
- There is a strong link between whether anglophones and allophones know French and whether they continue to reside in Quebec.

Part of the difference in losses between unilingual and bilingual anglophones may reflect interaction between the place of residence and the opportunities and rewards of knowing French. In other words, anglophones who leave Quebec at a very young age have fewer opportunities to learn French and may expect smaller returns to such an investment. To control for this factor, I examined the mobility of Quebec-born adult residents between 1981 and 1986 (see Table A-15). A bilingual-unilingual difference in the rates of residence remained, indicating that language skills are one determinant of the choice of residence of Quebec anglophones.

The loss of anglophones from Quebec exceeds the loss of the native-born for Ontario and even the Atlantic provinces, where, respectively, 88.9 percent and 74.9 percent of individuals living in Canada in 1986 remained in their region of birth.[4] Indeed, one can calculate that although anglophones represented 11.8 percent of the Quebec-born population in 1986, they accounted for 60.3 percent of the Quebec-born individuals residing elsewhere in Canada.[5] This

---

4 My calculations using data from Statistics Canada, 1986 Census of Canada, Public Use Sample Tape — Individuals (2 percent sample).

5 Ibid.

outmigration results in a loss of human capital for Quebec. This loss is accentuated by the facts that unilingual anglophones are better educated than unilingual francophones and that the anglophones who leave are better educated than those who stay (see Table A-16). The latter is also true of bilingual allophones.

Where do Quebec outmigrants locate in Canada? Mainly in Ontario (see Table A-17). Toronto attracts many of the anglophones, unilingual and bilingual. Ottawa, with its employment in federal institutions, draws francophones and bilingual anglophones, but not unilingual anglophones. New Brunswick is attractive for unilingual francophones.

In summary, the evidence is that anglophones, especially unilingual anglophones, are much less likely to remain in Quebec than francophones (see Tables A-12, A-13, and A-14). What part of the difference can be explained by language skills? No one knows, but I argue that the behavior of unilingual francophones indicates the existence of language barriers, and that the difference in behavior between unilingual and bilingual anglophones, given the difference in schooling (see Table A-15), indicates that anglophones prefer an English-language environment. More precise answers must await multivariate analysis of data with information on the dates of migration and of acquisition of a second language.

One should recall that francophones, even unilingual francophones, have been mobile in the past, as shown by their migration to the United States, particularly New England, during the 1840–1930 period in reaction to much better employment and earning opportunities than were then available to them in Quebec.[6] Indeed, they have also exhibited some international mobility in recent years. Termote and Gauvreau estimate that 17,000 francophones left Quebec to go abroad during the 1976–81 period, about one-third of the flow to ROC in the same period.[7]

---

6 See Y. Roby, *Les franco-américains de la Nouvelle-Angleterre (1776–1930)* (Montreal: Septentrion, 1990).

7 Termote and Gauvreau, p. 201.

An Analytical Framework and Language Policies

This section of the paper is divided into two parts. In the first, I present an analytical framework drawing on the economics of language. In the second, I put forward policies for Quebec based on the following premises:

- Quebec is foremost a francophone society, the only one in North America. A strong majority of its members want to continue using French as much as they do now, and they want their descendants to do so as well.
- Quebec is a small, open economy, with democratic political institutions. It is located on a continent with a huge anglophone part that has the highest level of real income in the world.
- Quebec residents are willing to trade some income against a greater use of French. In my opinion, the maximum tradeoff is in the order of 15 to 20 percent of the income attainable in an English-speaking society.
- The continued use of French in Quebec requires that it have a significant number of francophones. Thus, the share of the population that is francophone should be maintained in the postwar range of 80 to 85 percent, and the number of francophones should be at least 4–5 million, given the population of its neighbors.

The first premise, which is the most important, is based on the behavior of Quebec francophones since 1760 and on polling data, which show a strong preference for French. For example, 95 percent of Montreal francophones in 1989 (94 percent in 1979) believed that a Quebec resident should know French, while 88 percent (84 percent in 1979) believed that French should be the language of work.[8] Only 40 percent of anglophones from Montreal agreed with the last statement in 1989 (25 percent in 1979).[9]

---

8 Paul Béland, *L'usage du français au travail: situations et tendances* (Quebec: Conseil de la langue française, 1991), p. 107.

9 Ibid., p. 111.

Notice that this premise does not imply that French is a better language than English — indeed, it is costlier for Quebec. Rather, it reflects preferences that are the result of both taste and transition costs. The need for a public policy in this context reflects the supra-collective nature of language, a skill whose value for one individual increases with the number of other people with whom it allows communication.

An Analytical Framework

Drawing on the existing literature on the economics of language,[10] I put forward the following propositions:

*   Societies, faced with scarce resources and competing needs, should minimize the amount of resources used in both internal and external communications while maximizing the benefits derived from such communications.
*   A society can maximize its net benefits by adopting a single language for internal communication. Doing so reduces acquisition costs by ensuring maximum economies of scale in the production of learning resources — books, teachers, and so on — and by ensuring an homogeneous, efficient learning environment in which all speakers know the language of schooling. Moreover, the benefits of acquiring the language are increased since it is widely used in the society.
*   For external communications, a society faces a problem that may be less or more complex. No issue arises if the society does not exchange goods, services, and ideas — that is, if it is autarkic — or if its internal language can be used in all external relations. If, however, the language of external relations cannot be the language of internal communications, several issues arise. How many languages are used in these relations: one or more than

10 For a partial survey, see François Vaillancourt, "The Economics of Language and Language Planning," *Language Problems and Language Planning* 7 (1983): 162–178.

one? Is there a dominant language — a *lingua franca* of international relations? How can the external language or languages be acquired and at what cost? In thinking about the last point, it is useful to keep in mind Simon's comment that it is much less costly for a society to acquire foreign language skills through immigrants than through training.[11] That said, it should be noted that language acquisition costs will be lower and quality higher if native speakers of the target languages are available to help in learning it.

What do these propositions imply for Quebec? First, Quebec is a society in which the mother tongue of the majority of the population is — and historically was — French. Thus, French should be used for internal communications within Quebec. Second, since Quebec is located in North America, most of its exports are to English-speaking markets; in addition, its technology is mainly North American and thus conceived and developed in English. Quebec should, therefore, equip itself with the capacity to use English for its external relations. Its North American location, with the resulting spillover of English-language cultural products — television, popular songs, and so on — and numerous interactions with anglophones, means the acquisition costs of English are low for Quebec francophones. Indeed, one may presume that they are among the lowest in the world. Third, although English is the dominant language in external relations, Quebec does interact with non-English-speaking societies, so it is probably useful for it to ensure some capacity to communicate in a few other languages.

The previous paragraph neglects some historical facts, however. Because of the 1760 takeover of New France by Great Britain, the use of English in Quebec was not and still is not the result of unconstrained choices. The presence of a large (though declining) anglophone minority means that English was and is used for some internal communications and that parallel networks of English- and

---

11 Julian Simon, *The Economic Consequences of Immigration* (Cambridge: Basil Blackwell, 1989).

Table 1: *Effects of Anglophone and Allophone Communities on the Francophone Community in Quebec*

Anglophone Community	Allophone Community
Advantages	
Reduced need for bilinguals and cost of investments in English	Reduced need for bilinguals and cost of investments in third languages
Increased interaction with North America and the rest of the English-speaking world	Increased interaction with the rest of the world (bilinguals)
	Reduced costs of social capital (anglophones or francophones)
Disadvantages	
Reduced investments in English by francophones (bilinguals)	Reduced investments in third languages (bilinguals)
Existence of parallel institutional networks (reduced economies of scale)	
Reduced utility level (unilinguals) (negative externalities)	Reduced utility level (non-French-speakers) (negative externalities)

French-language institutions exist for education, health care, culture, and so on. It also means, as Lacroix and Vaillancourt argue, that anglophones have specialized in jobs serving the external market and francophones in jobs serving the internal market.[12] This dichotomy may have led to an underinvestment in English by the francophone community when French-speaking anglophones were available, while paradoxically reducing the cost of such an investment. The presence of bilingual anglophones in Quebec also reduces the interaction costs between Quebec and North America by facilitating the exchange of ideas.

Table 1 summarizes the advantages and disadvantages for Quebec of the existence of the anglophone and allophone communities. One can see that bilingual anglophones — and, to a lesser

---

12 Robert Lacroix and François Vaillancourt, *Attributs linguistiques et disparités de revenus au sein de la main d'oeuvre hautement qualifiée du Québec* (Quebec: Conseil de la langue française, 1980).

extent, bilingual allophones — bring higher net benefits to Quebec than do non-French-speaking members of these groups. Indeed, unilingual anglophones, especially those employed in head offices, high-technology firms, or export-oriented companies and living in West End Montreal, can be considered part of an enclave-type economy.

Policy Choices for Quebec

One can imagine an almost infinite number of language policies for Quebec. My own recommendations are set out below, preceded by some useful rules for setting language policy anywhere and by specific goals for Quebec.

Two general points need to be made. First, the policies examined here are only a subset of potential policies. They exclude, for example, the wholesale compulsory transfer of non-French-speaking people from Quebec to ROC either unilaterally or in an exchange of populations with ROC francophones being transferred to Quebec. They also exclude the transfer of territory from Quebec to ROC unilaterally or in an exchange. In other words, West Islanders will not be traded for Acadians nor the West Island for Acadia. Both policies were used in Europe after World War II with about 20 million people affected.[13] I exclude them here since they are not advocated by proponents of a sovereign Quebec, and in my opinion, are unlikely to happen. Neither is any division of Montreal — especially since the only precedent of a divided major city, Berlin, has been overturned. Of course, as shown above, voluntary transfers are ongoing.

Second, the policies proposed below are appropriate whatever the final outcome of the constitutional debate. Recall that I have defined Quebec as a francophone society. As a result, the proposed policies reflect the language policy preferences of a francophone not fluent in English — the median voter in this society — for a French-

---

13 Joseph B. Schechtman, *Postwar Population Trends in Europe*, 1945–1955 (Philadelphia: University of Philadelphia Press, 1962), p. 363.

speaking society, as well as my own knowledge in this policy field. They do not take into account any legal or conventional "rights" of anglophones as such. Rather, they treat anglophones differently from francophones because of the former's better knowledge of English and higher mobility in North America. Anglophones contribute to the well-being of Quebec in the medium to long term only if they are fairly fluent in French and thus make fully available their skills and expertise to Quebec. Unilingual anglophones do not contribute to the welfare of Quebec in the medium to long term, though they may make a contribution in the short term. Hence, the policies elaborated here are mainly for individuals who reside in Quebec for at least one year, but the needs of short-term residents are addressed where appropriate.

Rules for Language Policies

Language policies should take three rules into account.

- Language policies can require the learning of a common language but should not prohibit the learning of other languages. Such a prohibition has no economic basis and reduces both the human capital stock and the welfare of the group affected. It is usually imposed to bring about cultural assimilation, rather than economic integration. The teaching of noncommon languages should be funded publicly or privately depending on their usefulness to the society for both integration and international interactions.
- Language policies should allow the use of more than one language in written material — signs, documents, and so on — when requiring that the common language be used. Bilingual or multilingual written material offers a choice that does not take away from one language or another but adds to the welfare of the consumer.

- Language policies may prescribe the right to use a language in interactive settings — such as orally delivered services — but should allow the use of other languages, both parties willing.

The first rule simply specifies that a supply-increasing policy for one language does not require a supply-reducing policy for others. The other two state that demand-enhancement for one language does not require demand-suppression of others. Indeed, language policies should not prohibit the use of any language but should stipulate what language will be used in case of disagreement.

These three rules are derived from the general principle that economic agents should always be allowed the greatest possible degree of choice since additional constraints usually reduce society's welfare. Because of the supracollective nature of language, however, the imposition of some constraints may maximize the welfare of the whole of society while reducing the welfare of some of its parts. As long as the gains from doing so are greater than the losses, this approach is economically justifiable on efficiency grounds, notwithstanding its distributional consequences.

Specific Objectives

The specific objectives of Quebec's language policies should be:

- to ensure that French is the common language of oral communication in the internal Quebec market;
- to allow the use of other languages in combination with French for written communication — for example, on forms and signs;
- to allow companies to use the optimum combination of languages — French, English, and others — to serve their external markets.;
- to facilitate the learning of English by all francophones;
- to require or to promote the learning of French by all non-francophones, the distinction depending on their place of birth and age; and
- to promote the knowledge and maintenance of useful third languages.

Proposed Policies

In order to achieve the objectives just set out, the following measures, which imply tradeoffs between English and French, seem appropriate:

First, businesses and public and private organizations operating in the Quebec market should be able to serve their Quebec clientele in French at all times. In practice, this already occurs at least 90 percent of the time in private transactions. The problem arises in anglophone areas of Montreal. The issue then is whether the right of francophones to be served in French should be conditional on their specific place of residence or absolute throughout Quebec. I see no reason to restrict this right and thus to impose mobility costs on francophones who want to use French while living in an anglophone neighborhood. Therefore, elected officials — for example, the members of school boards and municipal councils — and individual employees of businesses and public sector institutions that serve the public — hospitals, CEGEPs, universities, and so on— should be proficient in French.

This policy would send a very clear message about the economic value of the French language in Quebec. Upon implementation, anglophone employees who do not speak French would have to learn it within a reasonable period — with publicly funded support — or lose their jobs.

Of course, businesses and services could still serve their customers in English or any other language if they so desire. Indeed, in the Montreal area, the Quebec government should ensure that public institutions maintain an English-language capability to serve short-term residents and tourists, and in the rest of Quebec, the needs of tourists should be taken into account. Most short-term unilingual anglophone residents are in Montreal, yielding a critical mass of such individuals and thus explaining the different treatment proposed for this region.

Public sector organizations operating in English and controlled by anglophones should also be maintained in the Montreal area. Their size should reflect the size of the community that is anglophone (by mother tongue) in that region. Anglophones outside

Montreal should see these institutions phased out over a five- to ten-year period.

Given anglophones' higher potential for outmigration, postsecondary institutions should charge all students fees that fully reflect the costs of the degrees granted with *ex post* rebates paid to Quebec residents. Note also that the existence of English-language postsecondary institutions makes it easier for bilingual francophones to gain access to equivalent institutions elsewhere in North America by easing reciprocal access to Quebec in fields such as medical training.

Second, signs, labels, and forms should be in French but could also be in one or more other language(s). (Signs should be at least one-half in French.) This policy would provide suitable visibility for those languages yet take nothing away from French.

Third, francization programs would be maintained, but requirements relating to the use of French could be altered over time as technologies and markets evolve. The goal should be not the maximum but the *optimum* use of French — that is, a level of use that maximizes both private interest (profits) and public benefits (externalities). One implication may be a greater use of English in serving external markets.

Fourth, francophones and allophones, wherever they were born, would be required to attend French elementary and secondary schools, but during one or two years of their senior primary grades (grades 4 to 6) they could enroll in an English immersion program, which would give youngsters a better opportunity to learn English than they now have. The senior primary grades were selected since it is generally agreed that learning a second language early is easier (neuropsychologically speaking) and less costly (alternative uses) than learning it later, but there would no longer be English schooling in the junior grades (see point 5 below). Full immersion, as opposed to half-and-half bilingual schooling, is proposed since I believe that the former works better.

This policy would enhance economic opportunities for Quebec francophones. It would also create employment opportunities for anglophone teachers who might become unemployed as a result of the policies in point 5.

Fifth, anglophone children born in Quebec would be required to take the junior primary grades (kindergarten through grade 3) and the early secondary grades (7 and 8) in French. Early immersion is recommended, instead of middle or late immersion, since it facilitates interactions with the francophone community. This policy, combined with improvements in the teaching of French during the English-language years of schooling, would ensure that young people have a knowledge of French adequate to satisfy the requirements of the policy on businesses and services. The cost of such a policy would be low.

Anglophones of school age (primary and secondary) born outside Quebec would need to conform to this policy, but would, within one year of their arrival in the province, be required to attend school in French for at least three years. Note that in some cases this policy could require less French schooling of anglophones born elsewhere than of Quebec-born anglophones. This difference would reflect from Quebec's perspective the relative costs of various policies — for example, immigration and outmigration.

Adults (people age 18 and older) would have the opportunity, but not the obligation, to study French on a full-time basis for six months at government expense (living allowance and free courses).

This series of policies would mean that the requirement that individual employees be able to use French to serve the Quebec market would not be excessively constraining. It might also reduce population losses from the outmigration of Quebec-born anglophones who have not mastered French well enough to be easily employed.

Sixth, given the size and location of Quebec, there should also be policies aimed at retaining or promoting a subset of third languages.

I suggest American languages (Spanish and Portuguese) as well as Arabic, German, Japanese, and Mandarin, given the size of the markets associated with them. In some cases, it would be appropriate to link immigration and language (perhaps for American languages?); in other cases, target languages would have to be taught.

This set of policies would be appropriate, given the level and recent evolution in the socioeconomic status of French and francophones in Quebec. It would ensure that French is the common language within Quebec while respecting the visibility of other language groups and ensuring the use of appropriate languages in external markets.

The difference in the nature (optional versus compulsory) and length of second-language training for francophones and anglophones reflects the importance of French and English for Quebec francophones, with French as the internal language of communication, and labor market incentives and facilities for learning either language in Quebec.

To ease transition, the measures described in point 1 should be implemented with a three-year lag and those under points 4 and 5 with a one-year lag. Existing policies should apply to children born in Quebec before the date of implementation. The parents' language of schooling and place of birth would be used to establish access to English-language schooling.

Conclusion

From the perspective of a francophone Quebec, the presence of an anglophone community is desirable if it adds to society's welfare through a reduction in the costs of interacting with North America and, less directly, the rest of the world. This requires the members of this community to be fairly fluent in both English and French. Those who do not want to meet this condition have the option of leaving (or not entering) Quebec.[14] The least costly way of achieving the goal

---

14 Roger ko Chih Tung, *Exit Voice Catastrophe: Dilemma between Migration and Participation* (Stockholm: Stockholm Universities, 1981).

is by encouraging Quebec-born anglophones to learn French early, thus reducing the cost of acquiring this human capital and increasing the attractiveness of Quebec as a long-term location.

Whatever the constitutional status of Quebec in the future, anglophones' choice to reside there will increasingly require a knowledge of French. It may also be accompanied by an earnings premium reflecting the relative lack of language-based amenities — theater, and so on. Accession to independence would presumably be accompanied by a departure from Quebec of the remaining pan-Canadian head offices, reducing the size of the English-language job pool and thus making a knowledge of French even more important for anglophones.

Statistical Appendix

Table A-1:   *French-Language School Attendance*
              by Language Group in Quebec

	French Mother Tongue		English Mother Tongue		Other Mother Tongue	
	Primary/ Secondary School	CEGEP	Primary/ Secondary School	CEGEP	Primary/ Secondary School	CEGEP
	(percentage of group)					
1980	98.3	96.9	16.1	5.1	38.7	15.1
1986	99.0	96.2	17.6	6.8	64.2	24.1
1989	99.0	96.4	19.1	6.2	72.7	39.9

Source: Conseil de la langue française, *Indicateurs de la situation linguistique au Québec* (Quebec: CLF, 1991), tables 3.1.1 and 3.2.1, pp. 29, 37.

Table A-2:   *Schooling in French of Anglophones and Allophones*
              at the Primary and Secondary Levels in Quebec

	Percentage Studying in French[a]	Percentage in French Immersion
1980	33.0	9.1
1986	47.2	10.5
1989	58.2	15.6

[a] Percentage of students whose mother tongue is not French studying in French in either French-language schools or French immersion.

Sources: For French schooling, Conseil de la langue française, *Indicateurs de la situation linguistique au Québec* (Quebec: CLF, 1991), tables 3.1.1 and 3.2.1, pp. 29, 37; for French immersion, Statistics Canada, *Minority and Second Language Education, Elementary and Secondary Levels*, Cat. no. 81-257, various issues.

Table A-3: *The Use of French*
in the Workplace in Quebec

Percentage of Time French Is Used:

	By Francophones	By Anglophones	Overall
1970	87.0	17.0	77.0
1979	90.0	37.0	85.0

Percentage of Overall Labor Force Using French

	More than 90% of the Time	Less than 50% of the Time
1979	70.0	13.0
1989	73.0	9.0

Sources: Data for 1970 are from François Vaillancourt, "Le statut socio-économique des francophones et du français au Québec à la fin des années 1970," *Revue de l'Association canadienne d'éducation de la langue française* 11 (August 1982): 9–13; data for 1979 and 1989 are from Paul Béland, *L'usage du français au travail: situations et tendance* (Quebec: Conseil de la langue française, 1991), table V.4, p. 124.

Table A-4: *Montreal Newspaper Ads Requiring*
Language Skills for Managers and Engineers

	French Only		English and French		English Only	
	Managers	Engineers	Managers	Engineers	Managers	Engineers
1970	27	27	39	21	34	52
1979	36	43	44	37	20	20
1984	31	35	49	29	20	36

Sources: Data for 1970 and 1979 are from F. Vaillancourt and A. Daneau, "L'évolution des exigences linguistiques pour les postes de cadres et d'ingénieurs au Québec de 1970 à 1979," *Gestion* 6 (April 1981): 22–25; data for 1984 are from Y. Archambault, "Offres d'emploi annoncées dans les quotidiens et exigences linguistiques requises à l'embauche" (Conseil de la langue française, Quebec, 1991, Mimeographed).

Table A-5: *Average Employment Income in Quebec by Gender and Language Group[a]*

	Men				Women			
	1970		1985		1970		1985	
	Amount	Index[b]	Amount	Index[b]	Amount	Index[b]	Amount	Index[b]
Anglophones								
Unilingual	8,171	1.59	23,924	1.24	3,835	1.24	14,335	1.21
Bilingual	8,938	1.74	26,078	1.36	3,956	1.28	14,449	1.22
Francophones								
Unilingual	5,136	1.00	14,235	1.00	3,097	1.00	1,802	1.00
Bilingual	7,363	1.43	25,923	1.35	3,842	1.24	14,718	1.25
Allophones								
English-speaking	6,462	1.26	20,504	1.07	3,329	1.07	12,927	1.10
French-speaking	5,430	1.06	17,664	0.92	3,241	1.05	9,918	0.84
Bilingual	7,481	1.46	23,729	1.23	3,881	1.25	14,060	1.19
Other	4,229	0.82	12,666	0.66	2,343	0.76	8,539	0.72
Anglophone-francophones[c]	—	—	21,705	1.13	—	—	13,182	1.12

[a] Calculations were made using the 1971 and 1986 census micro data files for individuals with a positive employment income. The databases for the two years are not strictly comparable, since the 1986 census classified some individuals as having two mother tongues (French and English), but the 1971 census did not.

[b] Index = the ratio to earnings of unilingual francophones of the same sex (the reference category). For example, the 1970 earnings of unilingual male anglophones averaged 59 percent higher than those of unilingual male francophones.

[c] Individuals with both English and French as mother tongue.

Sources: François Vaillancourt, *Langue et disparités de statut économique au Québec: 1970 et 1980* (Quebec: Conseil de la langue française, Collection Dossiers, 1985); and idem, *Langue et statut économique au Québec: 1980–1985* (Quebec: Conseil de la langue française, Collection Dossiers, 1991).

Table A-6:   *Effects of Language on Employment Income in Quebec*

	Men		Women	
	1970	1985	1970	1985
	(percentage difference with respect to unilingual francophones — the reference category)			
Anglophones				
Unilingual	10.11	-12.76	0	0
Bilingual	16.99	-3.53	0	0
Francophones				
Bilingual	12.61	5.91	9.73	9.07
Allophones				
English-speaking	0	-21.01	0	0
French-speaking	0	-25.11	22.82	9.47
Bilingual	6.03	-9.08	11.10	5.32
Other	-17.64	-33.12	0	0
Anglophone-francophones	—	-9.87	—	0

Notes: For information on the database, language classifications, and the reference category, see notes to Table A-5. Calculations used a log-linear equation with employment income as the dependent variable. Other control variables were education, experience, experience squared, and weeks worked. A zero indicates a coefficient not significantly different from zero using $t = 1.65$ as a cutoff point.

Sources: François Vaillancourt, *Langue et disparités de statut économique au Québec: 1970 et 1980* (Québec: Conseil de la langue française, Collection Dossiers, 1985); and idem, *Langue et statut économique au Québec: 1980-1985* (Quebec: Conseil de la langue française, Collection Dossiers, 1991).

Table A-7: Management Positions Occupied by Francophones in Quebec

Study	Year	Percent of Positions	Year	Percent of Positions
Bernard et al.[a]	1971	72.5	1978	74.8
Sauvé/Champagne[b]	1975	19.3	1981	25.4
Vaillancourt[c]	1971	64.9	1986	77.6
Conseil de la langue française[d]	1977	38.0	1988	58.0

[a] Data for 1971 were drawn from the census; data for 1978 were drawn from a study of 3,893 individuals in Quebec. Individuals were categorized by mother tongue.

[b] The figure for 1975 was taken from Sauvé's data, which were based on a 1975 study of 104 companies with 1,000 or more employees in Quebec. Champagne's data were based on a 1981 study of 134 companies with 1,000 or more employees. Both studies focused on senior managers.

[c] Data were taken from the 1971 and 1986 censuses. Individuals were categorized by mother tongue; individuals classified in 1986 as having both English and French as their mother tongue were not included in the francophone group.

[d] Individuals were classified on the basis of their names using data from Financial Post Information Service, *Directory of Directors*, 1977 and 1988 (Toronto: Financial Post, 1977, 1988).

Sources: P. Bernard et al., *L'évolution de la situation linguistique et socio-économique des francophones et des non-francophones au Québec* (Montreal: Office de la langue française, 1979); M. Sauvé, "Les Canadiens français et la direction des entreprises au Québec," *Commerce*, September 1978; R. Champagne, *Évolution de la présence francophone parmi les hauts dirigeants des grandes entreprises québécoises entre 1976 et 1982* (Montreal: Office de la langue française, 1983); idem, *Langue et statut économique au Québec: 1970 et 1980* (Quebec: Conseil de la langue française, Collection Dossiers, 1988); idem, *Langue et statut économique au Québec: 1980–85* (Quebec: Conseil de la langue française, Collection Dossiers, 1991); and Conseil de la langue française, *Indicateurs de la situation linguistique au Québec* (Quebec: CLF, 1991).

Table A-8: *Ownership of the Quebec Economy, 1978 and 1987*

	Canadian Control				Foreign Control	
	Francophone		Anglophone			
	1978	1987	1978	1987	1978	1987
	(percentage of total employment)					
Agriculture	91.8	87.5	8.2	12.2	0.0[a]	0.3
Forestry[b]	33.4	92.3	28.9	7.7	37.7	0.0
Mining	17.8	35.0	18.1	40.4	64.9	24.6
Manufacturing	27.8	39.3	38.6	38.2	33.5	22.5
Construction	74.4	75.5	18.5	21.8	7.1	2.7
Transportation, communications, and public services	42.2	44.9	53.4	50.2	4.4	4.9
Commerce	51.0	57.8	32.0	34.0	17.0	8.2
Finance, insurance, and real estate	44.8	58.2	43.1	34.6	12.1	7.2
Services	75.0	75.7	21.2	21.6	3.8	2.7
Government	67.2	67.2	32.8	33.0	0.0[a]	0.0[a]
Total	*54.8*	*61.6*	*31.2*	*30.8*	*13.9*	*7.8*

[a] Hypothesis.

[b] The nature of the data for this sector varies through time in such a manner that intertemporal comparisons are difficult.

Source: F. Vaillancourt and J. Carpentier, *Le contrôle de l'économie du Québec: la place des francophones en 1987 et son évolution depuis 1961* (Montreal: Office de la langue française, 1989).

Table A-9: Language Skills of Quebec Residents (age 15 and older), 1986

	Anglophones			Francophones			Allophones		
	All	Unilingual	Bilingual	All	Unilingual	Bilingual	English-Speaking	French-Speaking	Bilingual
				(percentage of age group)					
All	9.1	3.8	5.3	80.8	51.6	29.2	1.8	1.5	4.1
20–24 years	9.8	2.8	7.0	81.4	49.6	31.8	1.1	0.9	4.8
30–34 years	7.8	2.6	5.2	84.1	51.3	32.8	1.3	1.3	3.9
40–44 years	8.1	3.2	4.9	82.6	49.2	3.4	1.5	1.8	3.9
50–54 years	9.0	4.3	4.7	78.5	50.7	27.8	2.7	2.2	4.1
60–64 years	10.1	5.8	4.3	77.1	52.2	24.9	3.1	1.8	3.6
65+ years	12.1	7.8	4.3	75.9	55.6	20.3	3.3	1.3	2.6

Note: Percentages do not sum horizontally to 100 because the data exclude allophones who know neither English nor French and individuals with both English and French as their mother tongues.

Source: Author's calculations using data from Statistics Canada, 1986 Census of Canada, Public Use Sample Tape — Individuals (2 percent sample).

Table A-10: *Birthplace and Language Skills of Quebec Residents (age 15 and older), 1986*

Birthplace	Anglophones		Francophones		Allophones			
	Unilingual	Bilingual	Unilingual	Bilingual	English-Speaking	French-Speaking	Bilingual	All
			(percentage of language category)					
Quebec	53.6	72.0	96.7	91.3	14.3	10.5	31.4	85.9
Rest of Canada	20.8	14.3	1.6	5.3	2.0	0.0	1.3	4.3
Rest of World	25.6	13.7	1.7	3.4	83.7	89.5	67.3	9.8

Source: Author's calculations using data from Statistics Canada, 1986 Census of Canada, Public Use Sample Tape — Individuals (2 percent sample).

Table A-11: *Region of Residence and Language Skills of Quebec Residents (age 15 and older), 1986*

Region of Residence	Anglophones		Francophones		Allophones			
	Unilingual	Bilingual	Unilingual	Bilingual	English-Speaking	French-Speaking	Bilingual	All
			(percentage of language category)					
Montreal	74.7	76.2	28.5	54.9	89.1	81.2	92.0	46.0
Rest of Quebec	25.3	23.8	71.5	45.1	10.9	18.8	8.0	54.0

Source: Author's calculations using data from Statistics Canada, 1986 Census of Canada, Public Use Sample Tape — Individuals (2 percent sample).

Table A-12   *Migration between Quebec and the Rest of Canada (ROC), 1966–86*

	Mother Tongue					
	English		French		Other	
	Number	Rate[a]	Number	Rate[a]	Number	Rate[a]
1966–71						
Quebec to ROC	99,100	133.4	46,900	10.5	14,400	49.7
ROC to Quebec	46,900	4.4	33,400	40.1	4,600	2.3
1971–76						
Quebec to ROC	44,100	124.2	41,300	8.8	10,400	32.8
ROC to Quebec	41,900	3.5	37,200	44.6	4,700	2.2
1976–81						
Quebec to ROC	131,500	177.5	49,900	10.3	21,600	56.5
ROC to Quebec	25,200	2.0	31,900	37.7	4,200	1.8
1981–86						
Quebec to ROC	70,600	108.2	45,900	9.2	13,700	35.0
ROC to Quebec	29,000	2.2	33,000	38.4	5,000	2.1

[a] Per 1,000 of the group of potential immigrants.

Source: Marc Termote, "L'évolution démolinguistique du Québec et du Canada," in Quebec, Commission on the Political and Constitutional Future of Quebec [Bélanger-Campeau Commission], *Éléments d'analyse institutionnelle, juridique et démolinguistique pertinents à la révision du statut politique et constitutionnel du Québec* [Background papers], vol. 2 (Quebec, 1991).

Table A-13:   *Probability of Quebec-Born Individuals Surviving in Quebec[a]*

	To Age:		
	20	35	65
		(percentage)	
Anglophones	45	19	7
Francophones	95	91	71
Allophones	89	77	56

[a] "Survival" means both continued life and continued residence in Quebec.

Source: M. Termote and D. Gauvreau, *La situation démolinguistique au Québec* (Quebec: Conseil de la langue française, 1988).

Table A-14: *Quebec-Born Individuals*
(age 15 and older) Residing In Quebec, 1986

| | Anglophones | | Francophones | | Allophones | | |
	Unilingual	Bilingual	Unilingual	Bilingual	English-Speaking	French-Speaking	Bilingual
	(percentage of language/age group)						
All	36.8	68.1	99.2	91.5	65.6	100.0	91.8
20–24 years	32.6	75.6	99.6	92.8	79.1	*a*	94.9
30–34 years	27.3	57.4	99.4	91.5	50.0	*a*	79.7
40–44 years	30.9	60.7	99.2	90.7	*a*	*a*	74.4
50–54 years	42.5	70.4	99.0	91.4	*a*	*a*	94.7
60–64 years	44.8	69.4	98.6	90.9	*a*	*a*	94.7
65+ years	50.1	74.4	98.5	88.9	65.3	*a*	88.3

a Sample is too small (fewer than 30) to obtain a meaningful statistic.

Source: Author's calculations using data from Statistics Canada, 1986 Census of Canada, Public Use Sample Tape — Individuals (2 percent sample).

Table A-15: *Quebec-Born Anglophones (age 15 and older) Residing in Quebec in Both 1981 and 1986*

	Unilingual	Bilingual
	(percentage of language/age group)	
All	41.7	72.8
20–24 years	39.8	80.6
30–34 years	32.0	64.1
40–44 years	35.7	65.9
50–54 years	46.3	72.9
60–64 years	46.6	72.7
65+ years	52.3	76.0

Source: Author's calculations using data from Statistics Canada, 1986 Census of Canada, Public Use Sample Tape — Individuals (2 percent sample).

Table A-16: *Mean Years of Schooling, Quebec-Born Individuals (age 15 and older), 1986*

Residence	Anglophones		Francophones		Allophones			All
	Unilingual	Bilingual	Unilingual	Bilingual	English-Speaking	French-Speaking	Bilingual	
Quebec	10.4	12.4	10.1	12.8	9.0	8.6	12.3	11.0
Rest of Canada	12.3	13.7	8.5	11.8	12.4	a	13.6	12.2

a Sample is too small to obtain a meaningful statistic.

Source: Author's calculations using data from Statistics Canada, 1986 Census of Canada, Public Use Sample Tape — Individuals (2 percent sample).

Table A-17: *Residence of Quebec-Born Individuals*
(age 15 and older) Who Have Left the Province, 1986

	Anglophones		Francophones	
	Unilingual	Bilingual	Unilingual	Bilingual
	(percentage of total internal migrants in language group residing in each location)			
Atlantic Canada				
Total	6.1	7.0	16.3	9.8
New Brunswick	1.8	2.4	15.6	5.7
Ontario				
Total	65.6	68.1	76.0	68.3
Ottawa	10.5	17.6	21.3	22.0
Toronto	29.2	30.3	4.3	13.1
Prairie provinces	15.0	13.0	4.2	11.3
British Columbia, Yukon and Northwest Territories	13.3	11.9	3.5	10.6

Source: Author's calculations using data from Statistics Canada, 1986 Census of Canada, Public Use Sample Tape — Individuals (2 percent sample).

A Comment

William G. Watson

It is hard to know how seriously to take François Vaillancourt's paper. The political climate since the failure of the Meech Lake Accord being what it is, many people apparently feel driven to take bold, brash, "so there!" positions. On the other hand, the author himself tells us in his acknowledgment that several of his ideas date back to 1982. Assuming the paper is not simply provocation for the joy of provocation, it is the sort of thinking that, if enacted into policy, would make many English Quebecers leave the province. Needless to say, it departs significantly from the soothing reassurances of both the Allaire and Bélanger-Campeau reports[1] about the maintenance of traditional rights. It also seems to me not typical of francophone Quebecers' thinking on linguistic matters.

The first section of the paper, which merely reports data, is interesting and unobjectionable. The data speak for themselves, even if Vaillancourt seems not to hear them (see the third point below). By virtually every measure described, Quebec is a more francophone place and the relative position of francophone Quebecers more favorable than at any time since 1760. The percentage of the population attending French-language educational institutions is rising. The use of French in the workplace has increased over the past 20 years; so has francophone control over the economy. Income studies show that "[t]he socioeconomic status of francophones and French has been improving in Quebec since 1970." If language discrimination has any effect, it is now working in favor of franco-

---

1 Quebec Liberal Party, Constitutional Committee, *A Quebec Free to Choose* (Quebec, January 28, 1991); and Quebec, Commission on the Political and Constitutional Future of Quebec, *Report* (Quebec, March 1991).

phones, not against them. Anglophones have been moving out of the province. All in all, if any community is dying, it is English Quebec.

The second section of the paper presents Vaillancourt's policy analysis. To my mind, this analysis is flawed in several important respects.

The analysis is essentially collectivist. Vaillancourt is concerned throughout with maximizing the welfare of "Quebec," "Quebec society," or "francophone Quebec,"[2] This is contrary to the individualistic tradition of modern economics, which would hold that, except in the geographic sense, there is no such entity as "Quebec." Rather, there are the people who live in Quebec, or if Quebec's government is to be studied, the people who currently make up, work for, vote for, or lobby the government of Quebec. Policy analysis conducted in this tradition would try to assess the costs and benefits of any given policy for all Quebecers who would be affected by it.[3] By contrast, Vaillancourt shows either little awareness of or concern for the quite significant costs that the policies he proposes would impose on English Quebecers.

If Vaillancourt's study has a social welfare function, it is perverse. Once policy analysts have calculated all the costs and benefits of a given policy, they weigh them using a "social welfare function." A social welfare function is a conceptual mechanism — which, in practice, is seldom used — for trying to compare different people's gains and losses. For instance, one can imagine that a democratic government might adopt a policy even if it produced costs for rich people that were greater than the benefits it brought to poor people. A government that acted this way could be said to have a social welfare

---

2 Thus: "Quebec is foremost a francophone society," "Quebec should...equip itself with...," "it is probably useful for it [Quebec]," or most chillingly, "the advantages and disadvantages for Quebec of the existence of the anglophone and allophone communities."

3 In fact, it should also consider costs and benefits for people who live outside Quebec.

function that weighted poor people's well-being more heavily than rich people's.

Vaillancourt no doubt would respond to the first point above that, in fact, he is attempting to do traditional, individualistic welfare analysis. If so, the social welfare function he is using places very low value on costs borne by English Quebecers. For instance, he is quite happy to abolish "over a five- to ten-year period" social institutions that most English Quebecers value dearly. In policy analysis of this sort, it is, to say the least, unusual to give groups low social welfare weights according to their ethnic background or mother tongue.

If Vaillancourt's study is cost-benefit analysis, it is lousy cost-benefit analysis. The policies Vaillancourt proposes would impose very significant costs on Quebec's English community — in fact, off the Island of Montreal they might threaten its existence entirely. But no attempt is made to judge the size of the benefits that would offset these costs.

The stated objective of the proposed policies is to ensure that the descendants of Quebec's French-speakers will be able to use French as much as today's do. The data presented in the first part of the paper make clear that if the trends of the past 20 years continue, future generations of francophones will be able use French even more than today's do. Although unique historical events are difficult to explain, it seems likely that past legislation in the linguistic area has had something to do with these trends, by encouraging both the assimilation of anglophones and allophones who remained in Quebec and the departure of those who did not wish to be assimilated. But even granting that it is existing policies that have made Quebec more French[4] than it has been since the Conquest, where is the evidence that even more restrictive policies are required to prevent

---

4 Or, more correctly, since we do not know whether the policies are responsible for this, "are not inconsistent with Quebec's becoming more French than it has been."
   Vaillancourt's emphasis on the fact that French was dominant before 1760 needs to be modified. It was dominant only for a hundred years or so before then. It is not obvious why a century's headstart on English and several millennia's lag behind the languages of the original inhabitants should confer moral primacy.

backsliding? The same goes for policy objectives based on a concern about income inequalities. The wage coefficients for nonfrancophones are now all negative. This suggests, if anything, that there may now be discrimination against nonfrancophones. What social welfare function would justify incurring any costs at all — let alone the high costs Vaillancourt proposes — to make these coefficients even more negative?

Vaillancourt ignores the problem of rights, except when francophone rights are involved. Modern democratic societies place especially high costs on policies that remove what are perceived to be rights. In fact, almost by definition, a right is something whose withdrawal is assumed to have a very high cost. Quebec's English community regards itself as having well-established rights in matters of language. Both the Allaire Committee and the Bélanger-Campeau Commission, deliberately chosen to reflect as broad a range of Quebec public opinion as possible, agreed. Yet Vaillancourt quite calmly proposes to extinguish English Quebecers' traditional language rights in matters of education.

Carelessness with people's rights might be forgiven if it were even-handed. A respectable argument could be made that in addition to the substantive damage inflicted by a policy, there is in fact no extra damage caused by its also having withdrawn what was perceived to be a right.[5] But someone who would make this argument about the withdrawal of rights from one group should not in the next breath adduce new rights for another group and then place extraordinary weight on any diminution of these new rights. Yet this is exactly what Vaillancourt does when he invents a new right for francophones — the right never to encounter a unilingual anglophone. To ensure that future generations of Quebecers will not have to go through such an upsetting experience — which, we learn, now

---

5 A respectable argument, but a wrong one. Withdrawal of the first right increases the expected loss from withdrawal of other rights that, because they were recognized to be rights, their beneficiaries thought would never be threatened. The attendant anxiety can be very costly.

occurs in fewer than 10 percent of private transactions in Quebec —
he is willing to go to extraordinary and expensive lengths. His goal
is nothing short of assimilating the last unassimilated anglophone,
even though the data presented in the paper's first section suggest
that under the current policy regime most unassimilated — that is,
not bilingual — anglophones will have either died off or left the
province in a decade or two.

The analysis is inconsistent. It is inconsistent in at least two ways. First,
Vaillancourt makes a point of stressing that "the goal should be not the
maximum but the *optimum* use of French [his emphasis]." This point is
one economists will understand well. Yet the costs he is willing to
impose seem incommensurate with any benefit they are likely produce.
To be precise, how would eliminating the last less-than-10 percent of
offensive private transactions provide greater security for the policy
goal he describes? And what would be the costs and benefits of
attaining this greater security, if, in fact, it is attained? In all likelihood,
the optimum degree of bilingualism would leave some Quebecers
unable to communicate with each other.

Second, Vaillancourt makes an impressive case for freedom of
choice in matters of language. For instance, he argues that "bilingual
or multilingual written material offers a choice that does not take
away from one language or another but adds to the welfare of the
consumer." Most English Quebecers would agree — though many
French Quebecers would not. But this statement seems to contradict
his argument about the "supracollective nature of language, a skill
whose value for one individual increases with the number of other
people with whom it allows communication." How is it that this
supracollective attribute requires constraints on oral communication
but not on written communication? I am not a linguist,[6] but I cannot
believe linguistics is so exact a science as to allow such subtle
predictive differences.

---

6 Nor is Vaillancourt, despite his strong convictions about how languages are best
learned.

The analysis is driven by distributional, not efficiency, considerations. To use the traditional language of economics, Vaillancourt's efficiency goal is to have more, if not all, English Quebecers become bilingual. As is often the case in economics, there are many, many ways of achieving this goal, ways that differ mainly in who bears the costs of change. It is not at all obvious that the least-cost way would be to have English Quebecers bear most of the costs, by, for instance, losing their institutions if they live off the island of Montreal or their jobs if they fail to meet linguistic standards after a six-month language course.[7] Positive inducements could achieve the same allocative result, though that course would require the francophone majority to share in the costs of transition. In the normal etiquette of making policy recommendations, economists are not supposed to decide matters on distributional grounds but instead confine themselves to efficiency considerations. In practice, they often transgress against etiquette. Vaillancourt obviously is no exception.

Vaillancourt's tone is astonishing. As an English Quebecer, an individualist, and an economist, I find the following sorts of expressions both repugnant and chilling:

- "Anglophones contribute to the well-being of Quebec in the medium to long term only if they are fairly fluent in French.... Unilingual anglophones do not contribute to the welfare of Quebec in the medium to long term."
- "From the perspective of a francophone Quebec, the presence of an anglophone community is desirable if it adds to society's welfare through a reduction in the costs of interacting with North America and, less directly, the rest of the world."

I am not a francophone myself but have lived in Quebec all my life. The francophone Quebec view Vaillancourt describes has more to do with the analytic tradition of totalitarianism than it does with what most francophone Quebecers actually believe.[8] Does he seri-

---

7 Which, I do understand, would be financed by the Quebec government.

ously argue that francophone Quebec does not value the diversity and dignity of communities or respect communities' historical rights? Does francophone Quebec truly tolerate minorities only if they are economically useful to the majority? What would be the view of francophone Quebec if an English-Canadian academic adopted a similar view with respect to the anglophone majority in Canada — that French should be tolerated in Canada only so long as it was useful to the Canadian majority?

Does Vaillancourt really want to fire elected officials if they cannot pass a language test? If voters wish to elect a unilingual anglophone office-holder, should they not be free to make that choice? As for employees of public sector institutions, is it really necessary that every single employee be proficient in French so long as local public agencies in anglophone areas are able to supply services in French? Are francophones who have chosen to live among anglophones, in anglophone areas, really substantially inconvenienced by having to shift from a unilingual to a bilingual clerk?

Why not *consider the partition of Quebec?* Vaillancourt says there will be no trade of the West Island for Acadia. Would it not be more prudent to consult West Islanders and Acadians before making this decision? Acadians might not wish to live in a Canada without Quebec; many West Islanders — we cannot know how many without asking them — obviously do not wish to live in a Quebec without Canada. It is true that most of the population exchanges that followed World War II were disastrous, but that is mainly because the populations in question were not consulted.[9] If a substantial majority of western Quebecers voted not to secede from Canada, how could

---

8 Lest this be considered hitting below the belt, recall that it is Vaillancourt himself who raises the subject of "the wholesale compulsory transfer of non-French-speaking people from Quebec." Though he excludes expulsion from his analysis, it is astonishing first that he feels it necessary to do so explicitly and second that he is willing to categorize it as among the "potential policies."

9 It is also true that many of the border placements that followed World War I were disastrous, precisely because they ignored local preferences.

an economist who believed in methodological individualism possibly conclude that the boundary of Quebec should not be moved? Modern economics is all about self-determination.

Vaillancourt's comment about the failure of the division of Berlin is irrelevant to this argument. The example of Berlin teaches only that divided cities occupied by ideologically opposed superpowers do not work. But the separation of Quebec from Canada, most separatists assure us, could be a friendly, minimally disruptive event. Surely friendly governments interested in minimal disruption could work out reasonable administrative arrangements for running a boundary through Montreal, if that is where voters showed they wished the line to be.[10] Vaillancourt chooses not to consider such options because "they are not advocated by proponents of a sovereign Quebec, and in [his] opinion, are unlikely to happen." They are advocated by many other Quebecers, however, and if people such as Vaillancourt would not dismiss them out of hand, it is possible they would be adopted.

A final point. Vaillancourt notes that sizable voluntary transfers of population are already taking place. In fact, such transfers might be better characterized as quasi-voluntary, since, in many instances, English Quebecers are emigrating to escape what they regard as an increasingly hostile policy environment.

Should Quebec universities really have a dual fee structure, with higher fees for those who leave the province? Assuming education confers benefits on those who do not receive the education, if all jurisdictions were to follow the policy Vaillancourt recommends (and many do) the result would be worldwide underinvestment in education, which would be inefficient. As earlier, distributional considerations appear to be paramount in Vaillancourt's analysis. He is concerned that Quebec taxpayers lose when expatriate graduates of Quebec universities confer the external benefits of their education on non-Quebecers. That may be true, but it is immaterial to an efficiency

---

10 In this regard, see William Watson, "The Stay-Option: Self-Determination for Quebecers Opposed to Secession" (1991, Mimeographed).

argument in which what matters is not who finances the subsidy, but how large the subsidy is. Provincial governments do answer to people who care about distribution, and that is a good reason to allow federal involvement in the financing of education. Note that Vaillancourt says his policy recommendations apply whether or not Quebec secedes. If Quebec does not secede, should a dual fee structure apply to Quebecers who move to other areas of Canada, where part of the benefits they produce may yet accrue to Quebec taxpayers through the federal tax system?

This Horse Is Dead:
Stop Beating It

In sum, aggressive language policies may have been necessary in Quebec two or three decades ago. By all evidence, such policies have had the effect intended for them — to the extent that the English community of Quebec is now virtually a dead horse. Quebec intellectuals should stop beating it.

Separation and
the English of Quebec

William G. Watson

According to recent public opinion polls, if Quebec were to secede from Confederation, many English and allophone Quebecers would leave the province. What people tell pollsters they will do in given circumstances and what they actually do when confronted with these circumstances are two different things.[1] On the other hand, some 125,000 English Quebecers did leave the province between 1976 and 1981, and although other factors were also at play, what was perceived as a hostile policy environment usually had something to do with their departure. The English and allophones who stayed in the province then may have had a different perception of the provincial government's policy stance, but many would regard the actual act of secession in essentially the same way as the 125,000 viewed the possibility of secession. It would, therefore, be imprudent to dismiss the possibility of further large-scale emigration if secession does occur.

The purpose of this paper is to ask why English and allophone Quebecers might leave, to outline the effects this exodus would have on those Quebecers who remained, and to suggest measures that might stem the outward flow, assuming this was thought desirable by those who did remain. (It might not be, of course. When the prospect of anglophone emigration is raised, many secessionists seem to take the view: "good riddance.") My conclusion is that the best way to allay minorities' concerns would be for an independent Quebec to adopt some form of federalism. The most extreme form

---

1 As C.S. Lewis puts it, "Only a real risk tests the reality of a belief."

would allow regions of Quebec where antisecessionists were heavily concentrated to remain in Canada.[2]

Any attempt to talk about what life would be like after Quebec seceded from Canada is, of course, an exercise in informed speculation. One reason is that no one knows exactly how secession would proceed. Even if the whole scenario were known, however, it still would be difficult to judge what effects would follow. Economics, if it is a science, is a very inexact science.[3] If this paper does little more than make clear that we would have to know much more than we do in order to judge the likely effects of a "regime change" — to use the jargon — as comprehensive as Quebec's leaving Canada, then it may serve a useful purpose.

Why People Would Leave

If secession occurs, people would leave Quebec for a large number of reasons, not all of them economic. This section of the paper summarizes several of the most important ones.

Flags and Stationery

Suppose Quebec's secession from Canada involved nothing more than a change in flags and government stationery: Quebec secedes but maintains all policies and laws exactly as they were before secession. Federal transfers would cease, of course. But assume for a moment these are paid entirely from federal taxes raised in Quebec so there is now no net transfer to Quebec, and, therefore, there would be no real loss resulting from elimination of the transfer programs.[4] Would people leave?

---

2 "Allow" is used advisedly. These regions have as much right to self-determination as do the other, mainly francophone regions of Quebec.

3 Even if less inexact than many of the other disciplines that also (rightfully) claim a say in these matters.

4 Also ignore the possible gain to Quebec from eliminating the inefficiencies of spending and taxes that produce no net gain or loss.

Many probably would. As recent constitutional debates have made clear, flags and passports can be powerful public goods (or bads!). Even if life did not change much in Quebec following secession, many Quebecers would suffer a loss as a result of no longer being Canadians.[5] This loss might be large enough for them to sacrifice economically in order to move to Canada. How large this sacrifice would be and how large a sacrifice they would be willing to make are hard to say, just as it is hard to say how much Quebecers who favor independence would have to sacrifice or would be willing to sacrifice in order to achieve it. As already suggested, surveys on such questions generally mean little until people are actually confronted with the choice. On the other hand, many Canadians are at least as patriotic as Quebec *indépendantistes*. It is possible that emigrants would willingly undergo a considerable sacrifice in order to live in Canada.

There might also be second-order effects. Secession could cause at least some migration to Quebec. If Canada responded to Quebec's departure by reducing French-language services, as it almost certainly would, those who wanted such services for themselves or their children might move to Quebec. It is also possible that Canada without Quebec would not be as attractive to some English Quebecers as Canada with Quebec.[6] The result might be slightly less emigration from Quebec than might otherwise be expected, as well as, among those who did leave, more emigration to the United States and elsewhere rather than to Canada. (For the same reason, there might also be an increase in emigration from the rest of Canada to the United States or other destinations.) My guess is these second-order effects would not be large, however. It is more difficult to say

---

5 This point has to be phrased carefully. It might be that people would be permitted to maintain Canadian citizenship and to reside in Quebec as expatriates. But they could no longer live in Quebec as Canadians *except* as expatriates.

6 Writing about emigrants from English Quebec, Westley says: "Many of those who leave feel to some extent like strangers in other parts of Canada. It is a process of self-discovery in which they find that they are 'French' in many of their attitudes — or at least Quebecers as much as Canadians" (Margaret Westley, *Remembrance of Grandeur: The Anglo Protestant Elite of Montreal 1900–1950* [Montreal: Éditions Libre Expression, 1990]).

how large the first-order departure of disaffected English and allophone Quebecers would be. It might well be as high as one in two or three members of the relevant populations.[7] If the exodus were this large, both Canada and Quebec could experience substantial economic effects.

Fear of Economic Loss

Secession would change more than flags and government stationery, however. It would have little point if it did not. Quebecers who favor it presumably wish things to change or at least to evolve differently than they would if Confederation continued. Surely the fuss is not simply about symbols.[8]

Almost any number of changes can be imagined. For the moment, it is useful to focus on economic changes.

How Quebec's economy would fare under independence is obviously a matter of great controversy. Right now, the only certainty is that the small industry whose purpose is to answer this question would decline, since eventually we would know. In fact, the reality of what would happen — which this paper cannot hope to determine and, therefore, does not try — may be less important than what people *believe* will happen. There is a widespread, bedrock conviction among Quebec's English and allophone population that the relative standard of living in Quebec would decline, at least temporarily and probably permanently, after secession. In support of this view, those who hold it point to many factors, including the elimination of federal transfers and transfer payments, the likelihood of a chilling effect on foreign investment, the possibility of capital flight from Quebec as a result of uncertainty about postsecession monetary and political regimes, the likelihood of either an increase in Quebec tax rates or a reduction in public services, and so on.

---

7 In fact, a recent poll suggested only 35 percent of anglophone Quebecers would stay.

8 This incredulity is at least partly disingenuous. In my view, Quebec has no substantive grievances within Confederation, so the dispute must be about flags — though this obviously does not mean the problem is not serious.

It can be argued, as supporters of secession generally do, that these various possibilities are overblown: net federal transfers are not nearly as great as gross transfers, monetary and political regimes likely would be clarified early on in the secession negotiations, non-Quebec investors have investments in many other places where politics are much less stable than can be imagined for an independent Quebec, and so on. The merits of these arguments can be weighed at length.[9] What is crucial, however, is that they cannot be settled with any degree of certainty; that most English and allophone Quebecers are very skeptical of the secessionists' counterarguments; and that expectations, not emerging reality, will dominate the decision-making of potential emigrants. Emerging reality may well modify expectations as the secession debate proceeds, but a decision about where to live is a long-run decision, and people making it must take into account many events that have not yet happened. If they expect to suffer a significant loss in economic well-being as a result of secession, they are unlikely to wait around to see if their worst fears come true. In deciding whether to leave or not, they will be keying on political events over the next six months or so. How secession eventually went, even if it went very well, is essentially irrelevant to their decision.

In fact, this argument does not depend on the existence of uncertainty. Many secessionists concede it is virtually certain that living standards would decline in the immediate aftermath of secession. In their view, this is a reasonable price to pay for establishing Quebec's independence. Most English and allophone Quebecers do not see the situation as a tradeoff, however. Rather, one negative — economic hardship — would be added to another — Quebec's secession.

It is, therefore, reasonable to conclude that many English and allophone Quebecers would leave for economic reasons alone. How many is obviously hard to say, although, as noted, substantial numbers did leave between 1976 and 1981.[10]

---

9 Although this time round, compared with the pre-1980 period, there has been less debate about the likely economic consequences of secession.

10 This was double the rate of emigration from Northern Ireland over the same period.

Fear of Diminished Rights

Economics is not everything, of course, even to English Canadians. Another concern many English Quebecers have is what would happen to their rights and institutions following secession.[11]

Both the Allaire report and the report of the Bélanger-Campeau Commission try to be reassuring on this score. The Allaire report says that:

> Throughout its history, Quebec society has demonstrated profound respect for rights and freedoms. In many ways, Quebec has been a leader in relation to the rest of Canada. Quebec was the first province to adopt a charter of human rights and freedoms, in 1975. Quebec is a tolerant society.
>
> Quebec's anglophone community has always been able to fully exercise its right to express itself through social and cultural institutions that reflect its personality and culture. The rights of anglophones in Quebec extend far beyond the definitions of charters of rights and freedoms.
>
> Quebec recognizes that citizens of cultural communities are an asset and contribute to the wealth and pluralism of society. The Quebec Liberal Party has always adhered to the tradition of tolerance and openness of the francophone majority and has made sustained efforts to improve the recognition of cultural communities. In this regard, Quebec's record is amply positive and compares well with the performance of other western societies. The QLP intends to continue its initiatives, seeking out original ways to protect the right of cultural communities to preserve and promote their distinctiveness while encouraging their integration into Quebec society.
>
> The demographic situation will bring about an increasingly cosmopolitan Quebec over the next few years. Its sensitivity to the needs and specific features of minorities and the various groups that make up our society will be a very valuable asset....

---

11 Here the discussion is mainly about English Quebecers, since the rights at issue have traditionally been seen as rights they possessed. Over time, however, many allophones have joined the English community.

Not only must the new political order guarantee the same respect for every person's rights and freedoms, but it must promote the full development of cultural, linguistic and religious communities within Quebec. Specifically, it must safeguard the recognized historic rights of anglophone Quebeckers and specifically the right to their own social and cultural institutions along with the right to manage their development....It will preserve rights currently recognized by the Constitution of Canada and the courts....It will continue to guarantee the right of allophone communities to develop themselves as cultural communities. To protect fundamental rights, the Quebec Charter of human rights and freedoms will be entrenched in the new constitution of Quebec.[12]

And Bélanger-Campeau reads as follows:

The English-speaking community has been historically part of Quebec's reality. Its significant contribution to Quebec's development must be stressed and continue to be recognized. As a linguistic minority in Quebec, it is seeking, with French-speaking Quebecers who are themselves a minority in Canada, the development of respectful, harmonious relations, and this goal has largely been attained. A number of differences persist; both sides must endeavour to resolve them in a spirit of openness. With respect to the political and constitutional future of Quebec, it is important to maintain, in collaboration with the English-speaking community, legal guarantees which ensure the complete protection of its rights and institutions, and its full participation in Quebec society.[13]

Despite these reassurances, most English Quebecers feel they have reason to worry whether their traditional rights would be respected after secession. To begin with, most feel these rights have been substantially eroded over the past two decades. A traditional regime

---

12 Quebec Liberal Party, Constitutional Committee, *A Quebec Free to Choose* (Quebec, January 28, 1991), pp. 31–32.

13 Quebec, Commission on the Political and Constitutional Future of Quebec [Bélanger-Campeau Commission], *Report* (Quebec, March 1991), pp. 66–67.

of freedom of choice in education has been replaced by a regime in which eligibility for publicly funded English-language education is regulated. The language of work has been extensively regulated, and so has the language of commercial signs. Most English Quebecers also feel that the number of public services available in English has been reduced. Thus, even if the repeated reassurances that traditional rights would be respected are taken at face value, there is ample room for disagreement over what these traditional rights are. Using the traditional meaning of "tradition," the tradition in Quebec used to be that people were allowed to post commercial signs in any language they pleased. In the middle 1970s, however, this tradition was made illegal. Does "tradition" now mean "what is permitted by law at the time of secession" — in which case there is still time for further reductions in rights? Or does "tradition" mean "tradition"?

Though convinced that their rights have been diminished in recent years, most English Quebecers are not greatly dissatisfied with the status quo in Quebec. Many fewer left the province in the middle and late 1980s than in the 1970s and early 1980s. Because many English Quebecers are quite mobile, their having stayed is *prima facie* evidence that their dissatisfaction with their current role in Quebec is not excessive. If they could be assured that the cultural and linguistic status quo would be maintained after secession, they might well find this aspect of the regime change tolerable — though they might yet leave for the patriotic and economic reasons already described.

There is widespread skepticism within the English community about whether the status quo would be maintained, however. The idea that independence guarantees change has a compelling logic, since the desire for change is presumably its principal motivation. Secession would be the ultimate expression of Quebec's dissatisfaction with the status quo.[14] If the status quo is offensive, it follows that Quebec's majority would prefer public policies that the status quo

---

14 No words are spoken more scornfully by Quebec elites than "status quo" — except perhaps "Pierre Elliot Trudeau".

currently does not permit. Much recent discussion has focused on dissatisfaction with duplication in constitutional matters and with the alleged inability of Quebec policymakers to manage the economy the way they would like to. But most English Quebecers assume there would also be initiatives of one kind or another in the linguistic and cultural area. Even if most secessionists have no explicit public policy program in mind, the political calculus of postindependence Quebec seems likely to produce one, especially if the English and allophone populations decline even further. Hence there is an incentive to leave before the rush — an incentive that, of course, is likely to produce a rush.

Pure logic aside, a second worry has to do with a possible backlash in Quebec against changes that would be likely in English Canada if Quebec secedes. In a Canada without Quebec, only 4 percent of the population would speak French as their principal language.[15] Even if English Canadians were mainly indifferent to Quebec's departure, it is hard to imagine that federal government services to French speakers would be maintained at current levels. It is even harder to imagine provincial or municipal government services being maintained in French.[16] And, of course, many English Canadians outside Quebec would not be indifferent to its secession. Quite the contrary, they would be infuriated and likely to express their feelings in terms even more graphic than stomping on the *fleur-de-lis*.[17] Increased English-Canadian intolerance would not escape the attention of the Quebec media, with the probable result that

---

15 This neglects any migration resulting from secession. If the moves were mainly of francophones to Quebec, the following argument would be strengthened. It is possible, however, that some francophones might leave Quebec after secession, whether for economic or political reasons.

16 Except in New Brunswick, which might well remain officially bilingual.

17 The Spicer report quotes one English Canadian as saying "If Quebec separates there must be no sovereignty association, no economic union, no common currency. If Quebec breaks up this country it will be an enemy and one does not associate with enemies." Canada, Citizens' Forum on Canada's Future, *Report* (Ottawa: Supply and Services Canada, 1991), p. 60.

intolerance would also increase among French Quebecers. The country's twin linguistic minorities have always been hostages to acts of intolerance by their respective majorities. The fear of many English Quebecers, to put the point overdramatically, is that secession would amount to an agreement between these majorities to kill each other's hostages.[18]

This is not to suggest that francophone Quebecers are any more intolerant than most other people, English Quebecers included. But it would be a mistake to assume they are less intolerant. The idea that Quebec treats its linguistic minority better than the other provinces do is one of the distinct society's most durable clichés, and like many cliches is founded in truth. Unfortunately, it is most frequently invoked as an excuse for either reducing that minority's rights or ignoring improvements in conditions in the other provinces — that is, as an excuse for intolerance at home.[19]

Finally, even supposing no serious deterioration in relations between linguistic groups resulted from Quebec's secession, English Quebecers still would have reason to be concerned that their rights would erode within a separate Quebec. At the moment, several of these rights are safeguarded by the Canadian Constitution. For instance, the right to denominational schools was entrenched in the *British North America Act* and continues to be guaranteed by the *Canada Act* of 1982. As is well known, the Canadian Constitution has

---

18 In fact, there is growing fear that any constitutional accommodation that avoided secession would do the same. Two respected proponents of the "Swiss model," in which Quebec and English Canada each become officially unilingual, are Robert Young of the University of Western Ontario and John Richards of Simon Fraser University.

19 To state this as a theorem: because there is still a positive difference in treatment, negative first differences in Quebec are permitted, while positive first differences in other provinces are permitted to be ignored. It is interesting, however, that negative first differences in the treatment of francophones outside Quebec are seldom ignored, even those the Quebec government encourages, as in the case of the Alberta French-language education suit, in which the Quebec government intervened on the side of the provincial government against the French-language minority and the federal government.

often proved difficult to amend.[20] That has sometimes created problems for the Canadian polity, especially in recent years. But a constitution that is hard to amend is precisely what is wanted by a minority whose rights it protects. Among English Quebecers, the difficulty of amending the Canadian Constitution is, therefore, regarded as a virtue.

The Bélanger-Campeau Commission argues that the Quebec Charter of Rights provides extensive guarantees to minorities. This is not exactly true. The charter does indeed enumerate many protections for individual and minority group rights; moreover, the Commission established to enforce the charter has been active in doing so. On the other hand, the Quebec charter — like the Diefenbaker Bill of Rights — is merely an act of a legislature. It can be overruled by any other piece of legislation passed by the Quebec National Assembly, and it can also be amended or even repealed by an act of that Assembly.

The Canadian Constitution, by contrast, provides several minority rights that cannot be overridden by any legislature, and these provisions can be amended only by acts of the federal Parliament and at least seven of the provincial legislatures accounting for more than half the Canadian population. This protection is not perfect, by any means. Amendments are not impossible. But given the historical difficulty of amendment, the Canadian Constitution gives better protection against a capricious or mischievous legislature than the Quebec charter provides.

This concern of minorities that the Quebec charter is too easy to change could obviously be addressed by the founding fathers (or parents) of the new country of Quebec. All indications are that the constitution they would write would entrench a charter of rights, as recommended by the Bélanger-Campeau Commission. It would also have to provide an amending formula.

---

20 Though it has hardly been inflexible, as is often suggested. It went through a major overhaul in 1982. It has also been amended informally many times over the years as the country's various executives have collaborated in their different jurisdictions.

Several ways of rendering constitutional amendment difficult will be described later. For now, suffice it to say that when rights are guaranteed by a document that is merely an act of a popular assembly, any minority has good reason to be concerned. Some English Quebecers might stay and see whether a Quebec constitution would turn out to be satisfactory in its elements and sufficiently difficult to amend. Others, expecting the worst, would not.

Fear of Fiscal Strangulation

A final concern has to do with the financial wherewithal that often is required if a minority is to exercise its rights freely. English Quebecers regard it as their traditional right to receive education, health care, and other social services in the English language. Most such services used to be provided by the private sector or by local governments, and with private or local provision, English Quebecers could take matters into their own hands if they felt insufficient service — or insufficiently English service — was being provided. Now, however, most social services are financed by the provincial government, which answers to the National Assembly, which in turn answers to the majority population. As a result, it may no longer be in the power of the English minority on its own to secure the social services it wants. To some degree at least, receipt of these services in English even now requires the indulgence of the majority.

To be sure, it is difficult to imagine any provincial government explicitly adopting a policy of starving English-language social services. On the other hand, this goal can be accomplished in roundabout ways. For instance, McGill University — which the Michelin Guide to Canada calls the "bastion of Montreal's English community — has long argued that the province's funding formula for universities has led to significant underfunding for itself,[21] a point the provincial government has effectively conceded by changing the formula in response to the university's repeated petition. Several

---

21 Bishop's and Concordia, the province's other two English-language universities, have the same complaint.

theories are consistent with this single set of facts. One that is very popular in the English community — and that was even given public voice by McGill's principal — is that persistent underfunding was not unrelated to McGill's being the province's best-known English university. Many English Quebecers expect that what they regard as discrimination in funding would become worse after secession, especially if relations between French and English populations elsewhere in the country deteriorated in the aftermath.

Consequences of Large-Scale Emigration

English Quebecers generally feel they have several reasons to fear both economic hardship and erosion or even elimination of their traditional rights following Quebec's secession from Canada. In many cases, this fear would lead to emigration.

The most obvious effect of such emigration would be that the émigrés would be worse off than they would have been had secession not occurred. Had there been no secession, they might well have stayed in Quebec. Their well-being after secession would be, therefore, less than their well-being before it. Unfortunately, the well-being of likely postsecession emigrants does not seem to be a major preoccupation of Quebec policymakers.[22]

Policymakers might be more concerned about the possible effects of large-scale emigration on those who remained in Quebec. The effect of migration on the economies migrants enter and leave is, like many things in economics, a matter of some controversy. Add the great uncertainty about how secession would proceed, and it is very difficult to say with any exactness what the economic effects of an English exodus from an independent Quebec would be. It is possible, however, to outline the kinds of effects that could reasonably be expected.

---

22 Nor of François Vaillancourt. See my comments on his paper elsewhere in this volume.

Effects on the Private Economy

The effects of emigration from Quebec would act through both private and public mechanisms. To deal first with the private economy, those who would leave can be viewed in their roles as entrepreneurs, employers, employees, savers, and so on.

To take the simplest case first, suppose only one person were to leave as a result of secession. If this person, whatever his role, had been earning the marginal product of people in that role, then his departure should not affect Quebec's economy. He was fully compensated for what he produced. His departure would reduce local entrepreneurship, work effort, saving, and so on, but it would also reduce what had to be paid for that entrepreneurship, work effort, and saving, so there would be no net economic gain or loss for Quebec.

This case seems most useful as a limiting extreme, however. If the person who left had been receiving less than what he produced, then those who stayed behind might lose as a result of his departure. If the emigration was large, so that inframarginal contributors left, this, too, could produce a loss to people who stayed behind.[23] In particular, if there were significant scale effects in determining local output or the growth of local output — as much recent research suggests there may be — "stayers" could also be hurt.[24]

As already suggested, it is hard to know just how many Quebecers would leave following secession. But it is not outside the realm of possibility that the number would be large, perhaps even approaching 10 percent of Quebec's current population. If such an exodus occurred, the effects on the private economic activity of those who remained could be large — quite independent of any additional effects from reduced foreign investment, uncertainty about currency or property rights, and so on. Obviously, the size of the effect would depend on exactly who migrated. If emigrants were dispropor-

---

23 This may be a special case of the case mentioned in the previous sentence.

24 *This* may be a special case of the case mentioned in the previous sentence. The economists most closely associated with this idea are Adam Smith and Paul Romer.

tionately the managers and entrepreneurs who are widely thought to provide a modern economy with its dynamism, then the loss would be correspondingly larger. According to most statistical profiles, English Quebecers are not as specialized in these roles as they were a half century or more ago. On the other hand, because such people are generally more mobile than other segments of the population, they might well be disproportionately represented among future emigrants from Quebec.

A further possible effect concerns Quebec's future economic relations with the rest of North America, on which virtually all secessionists place great importance. Use of the English language is crucial to the pursuit of export markets in the rest of the continent.[25] The presence of a large, active English community in Quebec probably now helps in this regard, both because English Quebecers themselves constitute a substantial share of bilingual Quebecers and because their presence reduces the cost to French-speaking Quebecers of becoming bilingual. The absence of an English community obviously would not make it impossible for French Quebecers to learn English — they could still watch U.S. television — but it presumably would raise their cost of doing so.

Effects on the Public Economy

Most public effects of emigration operate through the fiscal system. Migrants usually are taxpayers; they also consume public services. If they have typically paid more in taxes than they consumed in public services, then they have been net contributors to the public economy and their emigration imposes a fiscal burden on those who remain behind. In order for each "stayer" to receive the same public services as before, taxes must rise.

Even if the exact identity of future emigrants from Quebec were known, it would not be easy to determine just how large a fiscal externality their departure would impose on those who stayed. The

25 In this regard, recent census results suggesting Quebec is more French than it has been at any time since the eighteenth century are not encouraging.

calculations are complicated, and the cost of providing public services can be hard to determine.[26] On the other hand, if there are fixed costs to providing these services — and it is reasonable to suppose there are — any significant emigration would add to the net fiscal burden of those who remained behind. Those who left had helped pay this fixed cost but had not added to it.[27] Their departure leaves the cost in place but reduces the number of taxpayers who must pay for it. Most government services probably do have at least some fixed-cost component. Running them at a smaller scale would increase the taxes that had to be paid by remaining beneficiaries.[28]

If the fiscal externality imposed on those who remained were large enough, then the process could be unstable. As key taxpayers left, taxes would rise for those who stayed behind; public services would not improve, so more taxpayers would be induced to leave, creating a further fiscal externality, which would cause even more people to leave, and so on and so on. There could be offsets to this process, of course. For instance, the price of local assets, particularly housing, would fall with emigration,[29] which would make the region more attractive to potential immigrants — though it would not please stayers who owned homes.[30] But any eventual new equilibrium might be at a level of general welfare lower than the region had to begin with.

Effects on Quebec's Political Life

Large-scale English and allophone emigration from Quebec would not be without its benefits, of course. According to one theory of

---

26 For example, how might you calculate how much of the province's annual roads budget a given taxpayer consumed?

27 By definition, a fixed cost does not increase when one adds beneficiaries to whatever service is being provided.

28 A problem that is well known in Atlantic Canada.

29 Housing prices are low in Atlantic Canada and a very high percentage of the population own their own home.

30 The price of Montreal housing declined during the late 1970s and early 1980s as English Quebecers departed. This made it easier for many French Quebecers to buy a first home, though it inflicted a capital loss on those who already owned homes. It also doubtless discouraged some English Quebecers from moving.

constitutional design, the purpose of a constitution is to reduce the transactions costs of political decision-making.[31] After substantial numbers of English Quebecers had left an independent Quebec, there presumably would be less disagreement about what its cultural and linguistic policies should be and therefore fewer resources consumed discussing them.[32] The same might be true in Canada. Of course, this gain would have to be balanced against the loss both to English Quebecers, who would be worse off, and to those in the rest of Canada who would be hurt by greater consensus about what Canada's language policies should be.

Although greater linguistic homogeneity might reduce political tensions within an independent Quebec, it is not clear that Quebec could only benefit by becoming a more homogeneous society. Why some societies thrive economically and others do not is not well understood by economists, but according to one school of thought, pluralistic societies are more likely to be successful than homogeneous ones in an era of rapid innovation.[33] I do not suggest that Quebec would cease to be a pluralistic society after secession. Still, Québécois nationalism is essentially an ethnic movement, which means that Quebec might well be less pluralistic as a result of secession-induced emigration. In losing substantial parts of its English and allophone communities, it would certainly have lost a stubborn lobby for pluralism.

If an independent Quebec did take further measures to discourage the use of English, this likely would have consequences for its

---

31 See A. Breton and A. Scott, *The Economic Constitution of Federal States* (Toronto: University of Toronto Press, 1978).

32 Some *indépendantistes* might add that there would be fewer resources consumed in communication, since virtually all Quebecers presumably would be competent in French.

33 Against this theory is posed the model of Japan Inc., which uses forms of organization thought to depend crucially on Japan's ethnic homogeneity. Although there is much enthusiasm for a Quebec Inc., it is not clear that the interventionist policy initiatives implied by this model are of any practical importance to Quebec. The U.S. Congress, which would be a crucial player in determining the economic fortunes of an independent Quebec, takes a dim view of Japanese techniques of industrial policymaking.

growth rate. Most immigrants to North America wish to live in English or at least to learn English. Immigration to Quebec is already at a lower rate than immigration to other parts of Canada. If potential immigrants perceive an independent Quebec as being even less hospitable to English than it is now, its relative rate of immigration could fall even further, possibly leading to a reduction in the rate of economic growth. To be sure, if immigrants to Quebec were attracted by the existence of a sizable and active English community to which they would eventually attach themselves, this might also threaten Quebec's cultural survival. But this risk must be weighed against the cultural consequence for an independent Quebec if its immigration rate declined even further in relation to Canada's, for Canada may be more open to immigration without the Quebec-imposed constraints that currently operate informally and would have been adopted formally if the Meech Lake Accord had passed. Even within the current constitutional regime, the federal government has recently signaled its intention of raising annual immigration limits to 1 percent of the population.

What Can Be Done?

Without attempting quantification, I have argued that if Quebec seceded from Canada, substantial numbers of English and allophone Quebecers would leave, a departure that could have serious consequences for those mainly French Quebecers who remained. Assuming an independent Quebec wanted to avoid these consequences, what assurances could it offer potential émigrés so as to keep them from leaving?

What Do English Quebecers Want?

First and foremost, English Quebecers want to live in Canada. Barring an extraordinarily imaginative constitutional accommodation, it simply will not be possible to fulfill the Yvon Deschamps vision of an independent Quebec within a strong and united Canada. Thus, if Quebec secedes, some portion of the English and allophone community is bound to leave Quebec, and there is virtually nothing that can be done to persuade these people to stay. Quebecers of all language groups who do intend to stay should take this fact into account in deciding whether or not to secede, since the emigration could have negative consequences for them. It provides little guidance for policymakers in an independent Quebec, however, since the émigrés' decision would not be based on the actual postindependence policy regime.

English and allophone Quebecers, like all Quebecers, are also concerned with economic security. Here there may be some room for influencing a second class of potential émigrés, those whose decision rule includes considerations other than where the Canadian flag flies. It would not be possible to persuade such people that there would be no economic cost to secession. In general, they are firmly convinced there would be a large cost. But it may be possible to demonstrate a desire to keep the economic loss to a minimum. What is required are pledges, not about Quebec's postindependence relations with Canada and the United States, since Quebec on its own cannot make good on such pledges, but rather about Quebec's own internal evolution following independence. Minorities are naturally interested in such things as the average tax rate after secession, the slope of the income tax schedule, the level of public services, and so on — questions on which most members of the ethnic majority would also seek assurances. Of course, promises in these areas, however heartfelt or well intentioned, can never be ironclad, since they depend on how the economy and polity would evolve after secession, which is hard to predict. On the other hand, if a Quebec constitution was in place at the time of a final referendum on independence — or, indeed, was part of the referendum question — and if it provided satisfactory guarantees in the area of property rights, unlawful expropriation, and public sector borrowing, and if it also provided an amending formula that would make amendment difficult, this might well provide reassurance to the fearful. In addition, the final referendum question could itself include commitments to honor Quebec's full share of the Canadian debt, to provide a transportation corridor to the Maritimes, and even to allow Canadian goods into Quebec without tariffs. These sorts of commitments would substantially increase the chances for relatively friendly negotiations between Quebec and Canada and therefore for minimal economic disruption following secession.

Reassuring Minorities

The same technique — adopting a constitution either before or with independence — could also be used to go beyond promises to provide real substance to guarantees for minority rights. The content of such guarantees has already been hinted at. English Quebecers would wish to maintain a variety of rights: their right to educate their children in English at public expense equal to whatever was being spent on French children; their right to their own publicly funded universities and social and cultural institutions; and their right to use the English language — including the right to put English on commercial signs.

The form of the guarantees would also be important. The least convincing form is the only sort that has been given so far: a general declaration of intent to treat minorities well. No minority in the world — including francophone Quebecers in their relations with Ottawa — would be satisfied with this. Moreover, as a result of bitter experience, Quebec's English community believes it has every reason not to trust politicians making promises.[34]

Moving up the scale of credibility, a constitution adopted either before or with independence could both enumerate the English community's rights and provide an amending formula. From the English community's point of view, if the initial list of guarantees

---

34 For a blow-by-blow account of the broken promises of the 1980s, see Reed Scowen, *A Different Vision: The English in Quebec in the 1990s* (Don Mills, Ont.: Maxwell Macmillan, 1991).

were satisfactory, then the more difficult the amending formula, the better. In general, there are two techniques for making constitutional change difficult.[35]

One is to adopt a very stringent but essentially nonfederalist amending formula: for instance, proposed changes might have to be approved by two-thirds or three-quarters votes of two or more successive National Assemblies, or receive two-thirds or three-quarters of the votes from all officially recognized political parties in successive assemblies, or get two-thirds or three-quarters support in a referendum or in two referenda held five years apart.

Even more satisfactorily from the English point of view, Quebec's constitution might provide for an essentially federalist amending formula. Again, several variants would be possible. One would be to divide the province into regions, drawn in such a way that at least some were primarily English-speaking, and to require that any proposed change be approved in all regions. Another possibility is that a federalist formula be explicitly linguistic; a majority of all voters registered as "English"[36] would have to sign off on proposed constitutional changes. Or an assembly of English communities — or English speakers — would have to agree. This sort of system would not be outrageous or peculiar.[37] It is essentially what Quebec seeks with respect to the current Canadian amending formula: that Quebec, the principal representative of the French minority in Canada, be granted a veto on constitutional change. If there are to be genuine guarantees for minorities in an independent Quebec,

---

35 Actually, there is a third approach: to have no written constitution, along the British line, providing constitutional inertia through the doctrine of *stare decisis*. Thus, an independent judiciary burdened by rule of precedent would maintain rights. But English Quebecers might be reluctant to place their trust in judges.

36 Presumably Quebecers would already be registered in this way for the purposes of school enrolment.

37 Comparisons with South Africa are always inflammatory — though less so than they used to be — but it is worth noting that that country appears to be moving toward a regime in which concurrent majorities of ethnic groups will be required in order to bring about constitutional change.

a similar constitutional veto would be the most effective way of delivering them.[38]

Federalism in an independent Quebec could go beyond constitutional amendment, of course. Language politics in Quebec have a strong regional dimension. The decentralist philosophy that is at the heart of secessionism teaches that one way to defuse these politics is to allow local governments to control decisions about language. For instance, in several regions of the province quite substantial majorities probably would not object to a system in which public services were made available in English; in other regions, the number of citizens who would want services in English would probably be significantly less than the 10 percent that has often served as a guide to language policymakers elsewhere in Canada.[39]

Taking these steps would not necessarily prevent a large-scale English exodus from Quebec. It may be that a majority of the province's minorities are first and foremost concerned with "flag" issues. Or it may be, given the time horizons for making decisions about whether or not to leave, that it simply is not possible to put credible guarantees in place in time. On the other hand, federalism for an independent Quebec recommends itself not simply as a device for minimizing the economic dislocations arising from English emigration. It is a useful device for governing all pluralistic societies. Once the national question was finally settled and the need to show a united front to Ottawa and to the other provinces had passed, many

---

38 It should be emphasized that this is what English Quebecers want, not what they necessarily expect to get. One reader of a draft of this paper noted that a veto is also what Quebec wants but so far is not getting in its current negotiations with English Canada. Several points can be made in response. First, the negotiations are not over. Second, if an agreement is reached, it is bound to include some form of veto for Quebec, though this may simply be a way of saying agreement may not be reached. Finally, taking Quebec's various commissions at their word, if there is true tolerance for and good will toward the English minority in Quebec, there should be little objection to codifying tolerance and good will constitutionally.

39 Indeed, federalism within Quebec would not need to be restricted to language matters. Regions could take responsibility for the delivery of all sorts of public services, with Quebec City providing fiscal equalization across regions, as Ottawa now does with the provinces.

citizens of Quebec might find that close supervision from Quebec City was not to their liking. What once were called provincial-municipal disputes would become more severe, with municipalities and other regional entities demanding greater power to make real decisions on their own behalf. The idea that power should be devolved to institutions closer to the people would only grow as Quebec's independence became more secure. It is not impossible that Quebec City would eventually be the object of the sorts of abuse to which politicians in Ottawa have long become accustomed. Sensible secessionists would realize that, whatever the cost of duplication and turf-wrangling, societies work better when they contain many centers of power.

Rearranging Boundaries

Sensible secessionists might also realize that their decentralist philosophy would also favor redrawing the boundaries of Quebec if that was what substantial majorities of local populations desired. The bedrock idea on which the secession movement is founded and according to which the sovereignty movement is justified in international law is that people should be allowed the right of self-determination. If substantial numbers of Quebecers preferred not to join in the secessionist adventure and if they were sufficiently concentrated geographically, then the same logic that justifies Quebec secession justifies these people's self-determination.

Secessionist hackles invariably rise whenever this point is made. It is not clear why. Even supposing it were universally agreed that Quebec would be legally entitled to its current boundaries if it secedes, would a sensible central government thwart the democratically expressed desire of minority regions to go their own way — especially if going their own way meant continuing the status quo and not joining in a secessionist movement that justified itself on precisely the grounds the antisecessionists claimed? And would other countries recognize Quebec's claim to self-determination or readily accede to its requests for easy access to their markets and financial institutions even as it quashed minority regions' claim to the same right?

The practical difficulties of redrawing boundaries can be greatly exaggerated. The world has abundant experience with international boundaries. If Quebec secedes from Canada, there will be a new international boundary somewhere between the two countries. For most purposes, it does not really matter where. In fact, in a truly friendly breakup, with a common market and common currency to follow, it would even be possible to work out ways in which the border could run down the middle of Rue Peel Street, if that was how the referendum vote split.[40]

Secessionists who argue, on the contrary, that there would be overwhelming practical difficulties in redrawing borders are caught in a logical bind. They customarily argue that Quebec's secession from Canada could be accomplished in a friendly, nonacrimonious way. But if that is true, then it certainly should be possible to come to sensible arrangements about how to run the border and where to put it. On the other hand, if the postsecession atmosphere would be so unfriendly that negotiations about border arrangements would be impossible, then — Catch 22 — Quebec's secession would likely be much more costly than most secessionists have claimed. And if, as a matter of policy, Quebec was not forthcoming about letting minorities decide their own future, then — Catch 44 — the postsecession atmosphere would likely be even more frigid and independence even more costly than is currently advertised.

Of course, many secessionists may have calculated that English Canadians in general and English Quebecers in particular are so phlegmatic they would rather move than fight (politically or literally) for their self-determination. If they are right, independence would not only rid Quebec of English Canada; it would also rid it of English Quebec, which has proved so troublesome a minority in the past. If this calculation is not correct, life in Quebec may be even less pleasant than the almost universally reviled status quo for at least

---

40 See William Watson, "The Stay Option: The Economic Feasibility of Self-Determination for Quebecers Opposed to Secession" (Mimeographed, 1991).

several years into the future. But if it is correct, as it may well be, and Quebec achieved both independence and a diaspora of the English, the result would be a victory of *realpolitik*, plain and simple. Rights and principle would have had nothing to do with it. Truth would not be served by pretending otherwise.

A Comment

François Vaillancourt

Although William Watson addresses an important issue, I believe his paper contributes little to the ongoing debate. To address the issue at hand correctly, I believe one must (1) define the English of Quebec; (2) determine the key parameters of their utility functions; (3) examine their likely responses to changes in the environment, such as sovereignty or constitutional protection. That done, one can (4) discuss the consequences of large-scale outmigration for Quebec. Watson's paper fails to examine (1) or (2) in more than cursory terms, although he does address (3) and (4), at least analytically.

Who are the English of Quebec? Watson does not explicitly define the English of Quebec by place of birth, by ethnicity, by mother tongue, or by language of the home. Implicitly, he appears to add together all 1991 Quebec residents whose mother tongue is not French. This approach is incorrect for two reasons. First, not all allophones use English at home or see themselves as anglophones. Second and most important, a substantial number of anglophone Quebec residents are not Quebec anglophones in any meaningful sense. They are anglophone Canadians residing in Quebec (ACRQ). Such anglophones were usually not born in Quebec, are much less likely to speak French than Quebec-born anglophones,[1] and for the most part are temporary residents of Quebec, usually Montreal's West Island (Toronto East!) who work in the head offices of pan- Canadian companies.

I argue that policies developed for Quebec anglophones differ from those developed for the ACRQ. Because it fails to take this point

---

1 See my paper in this volume, Table A-10.

into account, Watson's paper is not really useful; there is no reason for Quebec's policies to take the ACRQ into account since they might depart with their employment should sovereignty occur. (The author is, of course, free to study any group he wishes.)

What do the English of Quebec want? Watson informs us — with no exact references — of survey results with respect to intentions of migrating should Quebec become sovereign. No other survey data are used, so we are left with one person's opinion, Watson's, of what English Quebec wants. Yet, there are survey data on the attitudes of Quebec anglophones to constitutional reform, language policies, and so on. These data should have been used to help us draw a better picture of what English Quebec wants.

That said, I shall assume that Watson is correct in his reading of what English Quebec wants.

How would the English of Quebec react to sovereignty? What would induce them to stay? Watson provides a set of plausible answers to the first of these questions, including both tastes and income/prices arguments.

What I found missing from the analysis — and of relevance to the lack of sympathy for emigrating Montreal anglophones, presumably condemned to the horrors(!) of Thornhill, Ontario — was a link between the outmigration of individuals and of employment. A sovereign Quebec would probably lose jobs from pan-Canadian head offices — Canadian National, Canadian Pacific, Air Canada, the Bank of Montreal, and so on — jobs that are now mainly held by anglophones, often unilingual anglophones. Both the new population and the new per capita GDP would depend on the mean contribution to GDP of those who leave and those who stay and on the multiplier impact of the jobs that leave and the jobs that stay.

It is also interesting to note that the reason for emigration discussed at greatest length is the fear of diminished rights — that is, language rights. Setting aside Watson's statement that "the country's twin linguistic minorities have *always* [my emphasis] been hostage to acts of intolerance by their respective majorities," which is incorrect from a long-term historical perspective and contradicts the existence of so-called traditional rights for anglophones in Quebec, one is struck by the lack of economic analysis of the values of these rights and privileges and of the forces that have led to changes. Is the author implying that francophones should not have taken measures to preserve and promote French in Quebec? That there was no need to do so? That the current anglophone generation should have been compensated for the loss of rights and privileges acquired by their ancestors through the force of arms in 1760 and 1837? I do not know the answers to these questions, but it would have been useful to see the author make a foray into the economics of conquest and deconquest.

Having indicated why the Quebec English might leave, Watson puts forward various proposals for inducing them to stay, some of which are astonishing for a man of his practical bend. For example, he suggests that in its referendum question, the Quebec government tie its hands with respect to the debt and so on. Such a proposal suggests that Quebec anglophones want to maximize the welfare of "the Rest of Canada" (ROC). But if they are *Quebec* anglophones, why should they care? This takes us back to my point about defining who we are talking about.

Watson also proposes that Quebec anglophones have a veto on changes in Quebec's constitution. This proposal at least has the merit of being a Quebec, not a ROC, approach, but it is one that I suspect would not be accepted by Quebec's francophones. After all, they are seeking sovereignty to increase their autonomy with respect to Canadian anglophones. Why should they do this and then give away a share of that new-found sovereignty to a group attached to the old majority?

Finally, the idea of rearranging borders is not improper when one considers areas such as the Pontiac. But presumably the Labrador border would then also be subject to realignment. This is why it is probably easier to use existing borders.

What would be the consequences of large-scale anglophone immigration from Quebec? Watson identifies impacts on migrants, on Quebec's economy (private and public), and on political life in Quebec. His economic analysis is correct overall and brings out the main consequences of migration from Quebec. I must note, however, that although the cost to francophones of learning English would increase if Quebec anglophones leave, the contiguity of Quebec to ROC and the United States probably implies that this cost would remain one of the lowest in the world — perhaps the lowest. (Indeed, it is intriguing to note that most countries with English mother-tongue populations — Australia, New Zealand, the United Kingdom — are islands!)

One should also consider that the reduced value of homes would be transitory since the supply of new houses would adjust. It is probably construction workers who would be most affected.

Finally, in reaching conclusions about the relative attractiveness of Quebec as a place to immigrate to, one must be careful as to the state of the world immigration market and consider income differentials and adjustment costs, especially since immigrants could still learn English in Quebec.

Conclusion

Watson's paper is interesting but disappointing and sadly amusing. It is interesting because of the topic addressed. It is disappointing because the community studied and its preferences are not well defined and, as a result, the (correct) economic analyses not as useful as could have been. It is sadly amusing in that it is highly revealing (probably unintentionally) of the ongoing existence of Quebec's two solitudes.

Let me back up my last statement with two examples. First, Watson says, "In my view, Quebec has no substantive grievances within Confederation." I do not know what he means by "substantive," but assuming that it signifies something of an economic nature, let me remind him of one instance — the 1976 debate on the language of air traffic control. In that case, a federal body (Transport Canada), backed by unilingual anglophone employees, tried to ban French

from air traffic control in Quebec, thereby imposing English unilingualism in a field where the international norm is the local language plus English. This ban obviously reduced the economic value
of French to Quebec francophones in Quebec.

Second, throughout the paper, Watson refers constantly to the
rights (privileges?) of the Quebec English. Nowhere, however, does
he acknowledge that obligations and duties might perhaps accom-
pany these rights. Indeed, if one defines "tradition" as the situation
existing in 1951 (only 41 years ago), the implication is that anglophones have a right to live and work solely in English in Montreal
and to impose the burden of bilingualism mainly on francophones.

In closing, let me suggest that Quebec anglophones must continue to reflect on their place in Quebec, but in order to do so, they
must first decide who they are exactly. I suggest that a commitment
to Quebec as evidenced by an adequate knowledge of French should
be a key component of this definition if they wish to have a meaningful dialogue with Quebec francophones.

The Contributors

Marcel Côté is a senior partner of SECOR, a Montreal-based consulting firm specializing in strategic analysis for corporate and government clients. From 1987 to 1989, he was a senior aide to Quebec Premier Robert Bourassa. He then moved to Ottawa and in 1989–90 he was Director of Strategic Planning and Communications in the Prime Minister's Office. Mr. Côté is the author of *By Way of Advice: Economic Growth in a Market-Driven World* (1991) and co-author, with Roger Miller, of *Growing the Next Silicon Valley* (1987).

Yvon Fontaine, a native of Saint-Louis-de-Kent, New Brunswick, is Dean of the Law School of the Université de Moncton. He teaches International Law, and has a particular interest in constitutional matters. He was president of the Fédération des francophones hors Québec from 1986 to 1988 and, as a staunch defender of Canadian francophones, he has written many documents and research papers dealing with constitutional reform from a francophone perspective.

John Richards grew up in Saskatchewan and served as a member of that province's legislature during the first term of the Blakeney government from 1971 to 1975. For the first two years of his term, he was legislative secretary to the Minister of Health. In mid-term, he crossed the floor and sat as an "independent socialist." In his words, he has "since mellowed and rejoined the NDP." Trained as an economist, he currently teaches in the business faculty at Simon Fraser University, Burnaby, B.C. He has written on resource policy, labor relations, and public policy.

François Vaillancourt is Professor of Economics and Research Fellow, Centre de recherche et développement en économique, at the Université de Montréal. He teaches and conducts research in the area of public finance and also carries out research on the economics of language. He has published extensively in both areas. He is Associate Editor of *Canadian Public Policy*, and was a research coordinator for the Macdonald Commission. He has also conducted research for such organizations as the Canadian Tax Foundation, the Conseil de la langue française, the Economic Council of Canada, and the Law Reform Commission.

William G. Watson teaches economics at McGill University and writes a weekly column on public affairs for *The Financial Post*. He holds a doctorate in economics from Yale University and was the 1989 National Magazine Awards Gold Medal Winner for Humour.

Members of the
C.D. Howe Institute[*]

---

[*] The views expressed in this publication are those of the author, and do not necessarily reflect the opinions of the Institute's members.

Co-Steel Inc.
Pierre Côté
The Counsel Corporation
J.G. Crean
Crédit Lyonnais Canada
Crestbrook Forest Industries Ltd.
John Crispo
Crown Life Insurance Company Limited
Hugh A. Curtis
Cyanamid Canada Inc.
Thomas P. d'Aquino
Deloitte & Touche
Desjardins, Ducharme
Desmarais Family Foundation
Robert Després
John H. Dickey
William A. Dimma
Iain St. C. Dobson
Dofasco Inc.
The Dominion of Canada General
    Insurance Company
Domtar Inc.
Donohue Inc.
Dow Chemical Canada Inc.
Du Pont Canada Inc.
Edper Investments Ltd.
The Empire Life Insurance Company
Encor Inc.
Energy & Chemical Workers Union
H.E. English
ENSIS Corporation
Ernst & Young
Falconbridge Limited
Ronald J. Farano, Q.C.
Field & Field Perraton Masuch
First Boston Canada
First Marathon Securities Limited
Aaron M. Fish
Fishery Products International Limited
Ford Motor Company of Canada, Limited
Formula Growth Limited
Four Seasons Hotels Limited
GSW Inc.
Gaz Métropolitain, Inc.
General Electric Canada Inc.
General Motors of Canada Limited
Gluskin Sheff + Associates Inc.

The Great-West Life Assurance Company
Morton Gross
Le Groupe Commerce, compagnie
    d'assurances
Le Groupe Secor Inc.
Groupe Sobeco Inc.
Gulf Canada Resources Limited
H. Anthony Hampson
Hawker Siddeley Canada Inc.
Hewlett-Packard (Canada) Ltd.
Home Oil Company Limited
Gordon Homer
Honeywell Limited
The Horsham Corporation
Hydro-Québec
IBM Canada Ltd.
Imasco Limited
Imperial Oil Limited
Inco Limited
The Independent Petroleum Association
    of Canada
Inland Cement Limited
The Insurance Bureau of Canada
Interprovincial Pipe Line Company
The Investors Group
IPSCO Incorporated
Tsutomu Iwasaki
John A. Jacobson
Jarislowsky, Fraser & Company
Robert Johnstone
LAC Minerals Ltd.
R.William Lawson
Jacques Lefebvre
David Lewis
Gérard Limoges
Daniel Lobb
London Life Insurance Company
Pierre Lortie
J.W. (Wes) MacAleer
McCallum Hill Companies
MacDonald, Dettwiler & Associates Ltd.
Robert M. MacIntosh
McKinsey & Company
Maclab Enterprises
James Maclaren Industries Inc.
Maclean-Hunter Limited
Charles McMillan

McMillan, Binch
MacMillan Bloedel Limited
William Mackness
Manufacturers Hanover Bank of Canada
The Manufacturers Life Insurance
Company
Maple Leaf Foods Inc.
Georg Marais
Maritime Telegraph & Telephone
Company, Limited
Marsh & McLennan Limited
The Mercantile and General Reinsurance
Company of Canada
William M. Mercer Limited
Merck Frosst Canada Inc.
Ronald H. Meredith-Jones
Miles Canada Inc.
Les Minoteries Ogilvie Ltée.
Robert Mitchell Inc.
Mitsui & Co. (Canada) Ltd.
The Molson Companies Limited
Monsanto Canada Inc.
Montréal Trust Company of Canada
Moore Corporation Limited
The Mutual Life Assurance Company of
Canada
NCR Canada Ltd.
National Trust
National Westminster Bank of Canada
Nesbitt Thomson Deacon
Noranda Forest Inc.
Noranda Inc.
North American Life Assurance Company
North Canadian Oils Limited
Northern Telecom Limited
Northwood Pulp and Timber Limited
NOVA Corporation of Alberta
Ontario Hydro
The Oshawa Group Limited
PanCanadian Petroleum Limited
Peat Marwick Thorne
Lucie Pépin
Petro-Canada Inc.
Les Placements T.A.L. Ltée.
Placer Dome Inc.
David A. Potts
Power Corporation of Canada
Pratt & Whitney Canada Inc.

Price Waterhouse & Co.
J. Robert S. Prichard
Procor Limited
ProGas Limited
Provigo Inc.
Quebec and Ontario Paper Company
Limited
RBC Dominion Securities Inc.
Redpath Industries Limited
Simon S. Reisman
Henri Remmer
Retail Council of Canada
Grant L. Reuber
R.T. Riley
Robin Hood Multifoods Inc.
Rogers Communications Inc.
Rothschild Canada Inc.
The Royal Bank of Canada
Royal Insurance Company of Canada
Royal Trust
St. Lawrence Cement Inc.
Sandwell Inc.
Saskoil
Guylaine Saucier
André Saumier
The Hon. Maurice Sauvé
Sceptre Investment Counsel
Sceptre Resources Limited
Dick Schmeelk
ScotiaMcLeod Inc.
Sears Canada Inc.
Sharwood and Company
Shell Canada Limited
Sherritt Gordon Limited
Sidbec-Dosco Inc.
Le Soleil
Southam Inc.
Derek J. Speirs
Philip Spencer, Q.C.
Standard Life Assurance Company
Stikeman, Elliott, Advocates
Strategico Inc.
Sun Life Assurance Company of Canada
Suncor Inc.
Swiss Bank Corporation (Canada)
Teck Corporation
Laurent Thibault

Publications in "The Canada Round"

The Economics of Constitutional Renewal

How Shall We Govern the Governor? A Critique of the Governance of the Bank of Canada, The Canada Round 1, by David E.W. Laidler (38 pp.; May 1991).

In Praise of Renewed Federalism, The Canada Round 2, by Thomas J. Courchene (102 pp.; July 1991). This publication is also available in French.

From East and West : Regional Views on Reconfederation, The Canada Round 6, by Norman Cameron, E.J. Chambers, Derek Hum, John McCallum, Doug May, M.B. Percy, Dane Rowlands, and Wayne Simpson (122 pp.; December 1991).

Europe Uniting: The EC Model and Canada's Constitutional Debate, The Canada Round 7, by G. Bruce Doern (52 pp.; January 1992).

A Social Charter for Canada? Perspectives on the Constitutional Entrenchment of Social Rights, The Canada Round 9, by Havi Echenberg, Arthur Milner, John Myles, Lars Osberg, Shelley Phipps, John Richards, and William B.P. Robson (124 pp.; February 1992).

Survival: Official Language Rights in Canada, The Canada Round 10, by John Richards, François Vaillancourt, and William G. Watson, with Marcel Côté and Yvon Fontaine (140 pp.; April 1992).

(Forthcoming)

Dividing the Spoils: The Federal-Provincial Allocation of Taxing Powers, The Canada Round 11, by Irene K. Ip and Jack M. Mintz, with Claude Forget.

Delivering the Goods: The Federal-Provincial Division of Spending Powers, The Canada Round 12, by Jean-Michel Cousineau, Claude Forget, and John Richards.

Fiscal Policy: Deficits and Regional Coordination, by Herbert Grubel, with William Scarth and Douglas Purvis.